Tranquil Muslim Mom

How To Find Serenity As a Mother and Cope With Overwhelm

Zakeeya Ali

Independently Published

Tranquil Muslim Mom by Zakeeya Ali

How To Find Serenity as a Mother and Cope With Overwhelm

Copyright © 2022 by Zakeeya Ali

ISBN: 9798843193751

COVER AND INTERIOR DESIGNED BY ZAKEEYA ALI

ABOUT THE AUTHOR AND HER WORK VISIT ZAKEEYAALI.COM

FOR INQUIRIES AND ORDERS CONTACT HELLO@ZAKEEYAALI.COM

FOLLOW THE AUTHOR ON TWITTER AND INSTAGRAM @ZAKEEYAALI

BISMILLAHIR RAHMANIR RAHEEM

IN THE NAME OF ALLAH

THE MOST GRACIOUS

THE MOST MERCIFUL

Dedication

All praise is due to Allah SWT the Most Compassionate, the Most Merciful. May Allah SWT bestow His peace and blessings upon His beloved, Prophet Muhammed SAW his family, and companions. I dedicate this book to my beloved and only sister Safiya, my sister-in-laws, my nieces, my daughters, all my girlfriends, and the ummah of ummis worldwide. May the advice in this book benefit you, and may all your sacrifices as mothers be highly rewarded in this life and the next, ameen.

Contents

Preface

I started writing the Tranquil Muslim Mom book in 2016 and finally published it in 2022 alhumdulillah because life often got in the way. Writing a substantial book is already challenging, but with young kids, a big family, and homeschooling responsibilities, it was a monumental task. I struggled with finding time to focus and had to let go of my perfectionism to write error-free chapters. So I feel truly blessed that years later, Allah SWT gave me the opportunity and resilience to finish this book – everything really does happen at the best time!

How I Started Writing

In 2011, I began my writing journey on my brand new website. During that time, my months were crazy busy, sometimes more than I could even handle, and I felt like my responsibilities were overtaking me. I didn't have time for any hobbies, my health and needs as a woman were at the bottom of the list, my husband worked long hours, and our children were young and dependent. My parents had also passed away, my in-laws lived far, my siblings were on a different continent, and because we constantly moved to new states, I couldn't maintain friendships. One day, while filling out a medical form, I had no idea who to list as an emergency contact.

I felt isolated and alone.

Since I was also homeschooling my six children, all under the age of ten, my pressure was intensified. My memory became vague, my heart was heavy, and my stress level was high. I was not at my best and felt over-whelmed by motherhood.

At that point, I had to decide if I was going to give in to my desperation, or take charge of my situation and change my tactics as a mother. I shed tears to Allah

SWT and asked him to guide me through my challenges, then I started brainstorming. Being homebound with my little ones, my only tactic was to search online for coping strategies.

I found a few useful sites, but nothing that appealed to me as a Muslim mother. After thinking about the next step, I decided to create my own website. I figured if I couldn't find what I needed, I might as well fill a need! I started recording how I overcame my difficulties whenever they arose, then I shared my experiences with other mothers who were looking for solutions.

Over the years, I received comments and emails from moms who felt inspired and supported by my posts. The feedback made me see how we can enlighten others through our difficulties. The challenges of motherhood had afforded me the opportunity to pay it forward by shifting the focus from my situation to supporting others - our troubles really can become a blessing in disguise.

Writing This Book

My intention in writing this book is for you, dear mom, to use my moments of trial and error to your advantage.

To learn how to enjoy motherhood from someone who has been through (and still is going through) hectic days but has found ways to feel more at peace as a parent who enjoys spending time with family.

I hope you will learn and implement the techniques I share from the experiences that have helped me cope as a mother of many kids, with various responsibilities and constant new demands. I can't promise that your feelings of overwhelm will subside after reading this book, but you may change your outlook to take hold of your life and find your own solutions.

As I began writing this book in 2016, I was homeschooling my six children, ages five to fourteen, and my husband worked out of state, so we only saw him one week a month. Coping with everyday life with teens, tweens, and young children was extremely difficult without my husband around or any outside support, but I knew that Allah SWT had a plan for me as He has a plan for all of us and He never gives us more than we can bear. Our Lord says,

"So, verily, with every difficulty, there is relief" (Quran 94:5)

So I persevered with patience and prayer waiting for my relief to come and in the meantime, I took the opportunity as a grass widow (and while my kids slept) to write about how to cope as a mother without losing your mind.

Now that I have finished this book in 2022, I am still homeschooling four of my children, two are in college, my kids ages are thirteen to twenty, and my husband doesn't travel anymore alhumdulillah. My difficulties have changed and become less physical, but more mental as I deal with adult children and a whole new set of challenges.

These are the seasons of life and our good and bad times will fluctuate. But remembering that Allah does not give us more than we can bear will keep us going. I believe Allah SWT has put us in certain situations for a reason - in my case, maybe one of the reasons was to write this book.

Motherhood is an art. Art gets messy. But your picture can be a masterpiece!

Introduction

Why is this book different from other motherhood books? Firstly, it's catered toward Muslim moms – and you know how scarce it is to find self-help reads in this category!

Secondly, it introduces new concepts in three parts, so you have time to digest the ideas and not get overwhelmed with information. Think of it as three books in one!

Thirdly, I designed the companion *Tranquil Muslim Mom Reflection Journal* as an optional companion guide to this book. It's intended to help you implement the concepts more effectively and is available on *zakeeyaali.com* and *Amazon*.

Lastly, I formatted this book in an easy–to–read layout with a floral design, paragraphs instead of indents, subheadings, and bullet points, so it's not daunting to read.

The Parts of This Book

Part 1: How To Be a Peaceful Mother

In this section of the book, you'll learn what motherhood is all about, how impactful is your role, the fallacy and reality of motherhood, what makes a good mom, and the motherhood breakthrough.

You'll begin the journey of enlightenment by discovering numerous reasons to *accept your role as a mother with grace.* This mindset is an essential step in regaining some semblance of order in your life as a mom, which is why I wrote it first.

Part 2: How To Cope As a Mother

In this section of the book, you'll learn how to become a less stressed-out mother while maintaining your responsibilities. I share ways of avoiding feeling despondent due to your challenging role and finding a beautiful balance instead. I list the traits a mom should lose to become her best self and how setting realistic standards can make her overcome her troubles.

The way we think about our situation directly impacts our life. Thus, making a conscious effort to change your mindset as a mother will be emphasized in this section and across other chapters in the book.

Part 3: How To Thrive as a Mother

In this section of the book, you'll learn how to get to know yourself and why it's essential to do this. I share ways to avoid guilt as a mom and why your health is a priority. I also list numerous ways to thrive in motherhood that I compiled from my 20+ years of experience as a parent and mentor for women.

My dear sister, many of your motherhood pressures stem from causes you're unaware of. That's why, when you explore what they are, you'll be able to solve your issues and avoid being overwhelmed and exhausted so much.

Remember, only YOU can begin the process of changing your situation.

Why This Book?

I felt compelled to write *Tranquil Muslim Mom* because motherhood is essential to our lives as Muslim women. Especially nowadays, I feel that mothers need even more support to survive and thrive as wives and parents.

Sadly, many of us have lost access to the sage advice from our elders and the experienced mothers in our communities who were our guiding force. We are now relying on parenting books and mentorship for that guidance, especially in the West, so the focus has shifted.

How To Reap The Benefits of This Book

To extract the maximum benefit from these chapters, I advise you to read them in their entirety, as each section is filled with valuable tips for becoming a more tranquil mother. I say this because I know how many moms will skim or not finish a book as life gets in the way. Yet, we owe it to ourselves to seek innovative parenting methods and feel fulfilled in the vital role of motherhood.

This book is also a compilation of the articles I wrote over the years on my website when I began my quest in 2011 to offer support for Muslim mothers and wives. So if you benefit, be sure to subscribe to *zakeeyaali.com* for special member gifts and follow me on most platforms *@zakeeyaali* for frequent updates.

Lastly, if this book impacts you, but you need further support, you can book mentoring sessions with me at *zakeeyaali.com/coaching.* I've worked with numerous women worldwide for over ten years to significantly improve their lives as wives and mothers, alhumdulillah.

My dear fellow mom, you CANNOT and MUST NOT put yourself at the bottom of the list. Your role is way too important! Everyone knows the impact a mother's role has on the family unit and society as a whole. Mothers need to realize this honor and start giving themselves the pat on the back they deserve.

How To Find Peace As a Mother

PART ONE

Motherhood is intense, emotional, and life–changing. Some moments can make you feel like crying one minute and laughing the next. Often you feel elated, then despondent, tired then motivated, stressed then inspired, and all this can happen within the span of a day! It's not that you're crazy; it's just the reality of being a good mother.

You'll notice that when you socialize with other moms, the main topic of conversation usually centers around family struggles, especially concerning your kids. It's a natural occurrence because motherhood is challenging, time-consuming, and encompasses most of a woman's prime years.

So I ask, have you been honest about the hardship of being a mother? Have you told yourself being a mom is really tough? Have you ever broken down and cried because motherhood took a toll on you?

It's okay to admit that being a mom isn't easy. It's not only acceptable to acknowledge the difficulties of motherhood; it's healthy! More importantly, it's empowering to accept that parenting is tough!

Numerous Muslim scholars mention that being a parent is regarded as a burden in Islam, and parents can only endure it with sabr (patience) and iman (faith). Allah SWT knows the toll it has on us, and that's why the reward is so immense.

When you acknowledge this and direct your mindset to think this way, you won't live in a fool's paradise. Instead, you'll begin to feel at peace knowing the inevitability of having parenting woes.

What Is Motherhood?

Pondering over the definition of motherhood isn't something many moms think about. Does giving birth to a child make you a mother, or does nurturing a child make you a mother?

According to the standard English dictionary, a mother is both a noun and a verb. She is *"A woman in relation to a child or children to whom she has given birth."* The word can also be defined as *"To bring up (a child) with care and affection."*

In Islam, a mother's status is considered very noble, blessed, and holds weight even over the father's status. We know this through the words of our beloved Messenger SAW.

> "A man came to the Prophet SAW and said: 'O Allah's Apostle! Who is more entitled to be treated with the best companionship by me?' The Prophet said, 'Your mother.' The man said. 'Who is next?' The Prophet said, 'Your mother.' The man further said, 'Who is next?' The Prophet said, 'Your mother.' The man asked for the fourth time, 'Who is next?' The Prophet said, 'Your father.'" (Bukhari)

In this Hadith, we see how much our beloved Prophet SAW emphasized the status of mothers in Islam and how they're entitled to receive extra care from their children. Though, it's important to clarify that a father's role is also crucial to a child's well-being.

A dad should receive the required respect and obedience from his family, for he bears the burden of responsibility and protection for them. Modern society likes to downplay the father's role as insignificant, but this actually places a heavier burden upon mothers.

A Mother's Role Is Impactful

A mom often spends the majority of time with her children and has considerable influence on their behavior. She sets the precedence, and her efforts are far-reaching as it directly affects future generations.

A mother has also been endowed with greater compassion, endurance, and patience when dealing with children, so her fitra (innate nature) is nurturing, kind, and merciful. In this regard, when a mother raises her child with iman and a wholesome upbringing, they'll have the tools to be a devoted believer, a good spouse, and a parent who'll hopefully pass this on to their offspring. This kickstarts a positive cycle for the next generation to come inshallah.

Likewise, when a mother raises an unruly child, who lacks adhab (etiquette and manners), the cycle starts off negative and can impact the future generation to be less wholesome. Thus, as mothers, we must understand that our impact on our children's lives is LIFE–CHANGING and TREND–SETTING!

So let's embrace motherhood for the powerful force that it is and know that we're the essential caretakers of our family.

The "Ideal Mother" Fallacy

If you think back to your beliefs before becoming a mom, do you remember how you imagined motherhood to be? Do you recall thinking how you would do this one way, do that another way, and be so much more prepared?

We all had our ideals as single women and felt anxious yet excited about the prospect of raising our own kids after marriage. Some of us figured that we could implement our parent's child–rearing techniques as a start and simply improve on what they lacked.

But, when the time came and our first child was born, our parenting standards got a whole lot more realistic. Motherhood became more about keeping up than being a fantastic parent and it was much less glamorous than we assumed.

Even though we adore our little one with every breath, being a mom was more burdensome than we envisioned. As time passed, we looked back to our childless days and longed for a fraction of the freedom we'd taken for granted.

The simple relief of an uninterrupted shower, a phone call, and a much-needed bathroom break! We merely required a little peace and quiet now and then to ease our mental exhaustion.

Hence the toppling of our ideals began. Our false notions of motherhood shattered even further when reality continued to knock at our door. Each stage of our child's development and having more kids brought on new challenges.

At this point, we started to make excuses for our lack of perfection and fostered doubt in our natural abilities as mothers. Inane thoughts like, *"Maybe I'm not maternal enough"* or *"Motherhood doesn't come easy to me"* riddled us with guilt.

Some of us also compared ourselves to the moms around us, who seemed like the ideal version of a mother figure. You know, the ones who maintain a perfect balance of compassion and firmness and always have a batch of homemade cookies in the oven.

Feeling like lesser women, we believe we're not good enough in the relevant areas of motherhood. A sense of hopelessness invades our thoughts, making us lose confidence in our abilities and developing self-doubt.

This is a scenario that many moms fall prey to. I call it "The ideal mother fallacy." It can break you down by keeping you in a constant state of guilt and remorse, believing you're never good enough for your children.

Following this line of thinking is detrimental and can lead a woman to feel bitter about motherhood.

The "Real Truth" About Motherhood

Fortunately, being society's ideal mother is not what our deen portrays, alhumdulillah. Our worth is not measured by a standard of housework and meal planning perfection. The so-called "less maternal mother" label doesn't indicate a lesser mom. Some women just don't fit the cultural depiction of a conventional mother.

These moms may think they're insignificant, need more expertise, or aren't innately motherly – but that's not the case! When we look back at some great women in Islam like the exalted Maryam, Asiya, Khadija, and Ayisha (peace be upon them), we should take note of the traits they're remembered for.

Maryam R.A is known for her purity and strength in raising Prophet Isa A.S without a husband. She faced slander and backlash for this but maintained sabr and put her trust in Allah SWT.

Asiya R.A is known for her courage and patience in raising Prophet Musa A.S. She married the tyrant Firoun but remained true to her belief in Allah SWT even when he tortured and murdered her.

Khadija R.A is known for her wisdom and support as the first wife of the Prophet SAW. She birthed and raised their six children, and was a loyal, devoted, and patient wife. She supported the Prophet SAW when he went for long spans of time away to the Cave of Hira and especially when he was receiving revelation which was an intense time for them.

Ayisha R.A is known for her intelligence in narrating numerous Hadiths about the Prophet SAW's words and actions. She was a comforting wife to the Prophet SAW during his Prophethood, in his advanced years, and on his deathbed.

These amazing sahabiyat (female companions of the Prophet's SAW time) are all women of Jannah, yet their strengths didn't lie only in their domestic expertise. This is not to say that the tasks of cleaning and cooking aren't important as some feminists like us to believe. These are charitable acts we do for our family's well-being and to please our Creator.

However, we need to place *less emphasis* on making domesticity the focus of a mother's role or use it to measure maternal success. The way we live nowadays, with our high standard of living, excessive cleaning and organizing behavior, and elaborate meal making, is not what makes us great moms.

Our intentions should be like the amazing women in Islam who placed greater importance on being *supportive wives, nurturing mothers,* and *faithful believers.* All the rest simply falls into place.

Realizing What Is a Good Mother

In many ways, I regarded myself as an unconventional mom. For many years I thought I wasn't a good enough mother and, unfortunately, believed this even though I saw my husband and kids thrive under my care.

I had these thoughts because I didn't enjoy cleaning, cooking, and baking, and I'd cut corners to give myself time to focus on other areas for my family. I did a lot for my husband and kids throughout the day, yet I still had a ton of guilt to work through.

I felt like this because I would compare myself to my family, friends, and the women around me who seemed to give their families a much better lifestyle.

Whether making more wholesome lunches, cooking homemade foods, having an organized and squeaky-clean home, or serving dinner with dessert promptly at 6:00 pm, I assumed this domestic perfection was motherhood success.

Over time, I learned that being a good mother is not what we presume based on material and edible delights. *Motherhood is an attitude as well!* I've found that the most successful nurturing comes down to how your family *feels* about you. It's how you *positively* impact their lives and the *happiness* you radiate towards them.

Even mothers who think they aren't great housekeepers, bakers, cleaners, and cooks are just as maternal as those moms who are proficient in these areas. I discovered that my *alternate* motherly talents counted just as much (and sometimes more) than the typical ones, but in another way.

For example, I love just *being* with my children throughout the day. I enjoy laughing, joking, and reading books with them. I like seeing them learn new things and teach them about Islam and life.

As a mother, I would focus most of my efforts on enlightening my kids in their deen (belief) and adhab (manners and etiquette). I spent countless hours educating them and even developed a curriculum when I couldn't find anything worthwhile to teach them about Islam.

I called it homeschooling, but it wasn't simply that; it was me being a mother in another way. A mom who was a teacher to her children, like some mothers before me, instead of sending them to school to be taught. I finally got honest with myself and saw my nurturing role as so much more than domestic!

Looking back now without guilt-ridden eyes, I realize how much I've done and still do for my family. I've finally accepted that just because I buy cookies instead of baking them, I'm still an awesome wife and mom!

A big issue is that women don't learn what being a mother truly means. Sometimes our old-school thinking and cultural expectations can also make us formulate unrealistic ideas of being a good mom.

The sad reality is that we tend to miss out on finding contentment in our maternal lives and simply *enjoying* our family. These inconceivable ideals and silly traditions hold us back without us realizing what's happening.

So do yourself a favor, look in the mirror and acknowledge the great mom that you are. How do I know? The fact that you're reading this book on improving your life as a mom speaks volumes.

Dear mom, stop downplaying your value and own your worth as a nurturer!

The Motherhood Breakthrough

As mothers, we need to change our mindset first before anything else. We must accept that it's okay to be an unconventional mother. We need to set *boundaries* on what we can do and understand that it's *impossible* to be good in every aspect of our lives.

Next, we should not *compare* ourselves to society's idea of a mother because it's not what Islam promotes. We need to *accept* that we can't do what some mothers do, and those moms can't do what we do either.

Even though another mom's strengths may seem more conventional, our nurturing efforts are still valid. When we think in a boxed-in mentality, we feel constricted and stunt our growth as mothers.

Through this new acceptance, we'll learn to be content with our limitations, find peace with our choices, and free our minds from false ideals. Best of all, our children will still love us and feel glad to have us in their lives.

Our kids are not asking for baked cookies over store-bought ones – they just want cookies! Our one-track mind makes us worry about petty to-do's that really don't depict whether we are good moms or not. It's extra, it's great, but it's not necessary!

So, where did we get our unrealistic ideas from?

You'll notice it stems from being around other mothers who believe in these ideas and not from our children's demands (unless we've given them high expectations and they're old enough to know the difference).

Accepting Yourself As a Mother

10 WAYS TO ACCEPT IT, LOSE THE GUILT, & LOVE YOUR ROLE

There are ways to understand true motherhood and find contentment by graciously accepting your role as a mother. This acceptance can help kickstart your journey towards finding the peace and contentment you deserve.

I regard the acceptance of motherhood as a crucial aspect towards ceasing to feel guilty about what you *can't do* and being delighted by what you *are doing*. You may be thinking, *"Why is this a big deal? Of course, I know I'm a mother."* Well, I thought this way too, but even though I accepted being a mom, I didn't accept the challenges of parenting.

As a nurturer, I felt like a hamster on a wheel striving toward perfection. When I understood the vast aspects of being a parent, my mindset changed, and I found peace in my motherhood journey. Here are ten ways of learning to accept motherhood to feel more blessed and less stressed.

1. Accept That Motherhood Is Your God-Given Role

Motherhood is a noble responsibility that affects a whole society. It's a blessing that Allah SWT has placed upon you, and He doesn't bestow the gift of motherhood upon every woman. He chose YOU to play a part in the circle of life and leave your mark on the world.

Do you see the honor in this dear mom?

The gift of motherhood comes with a multitude of responsibilities, just like any other part of society. When you learn to accept your role as a mother, you understand an ethical code of conduct binds you.

You've committed to giving up much of your freedom to take on the most significant responsibility of your life – raising kids! When you accept motherhood as your full-time job for the sake of Allah SWT, you'll feel honored to raise the next generation of Muslim adults.

To bear the weight of motherhood is hefty, no doubt, but you'll earn merit with your Creator for all this in the end. The role of motherhood may not always be easy, but your acceptance and understanding will give you the endurance to persevere. The Prophet SAW said:

"Every one of you is a shepherd and is responsible for his flock. The leader of people is a guardian and is responsible for his subjects. A man is the guardian of his family and he is responsible for them. A woman is the guardian of her husband's home and his children, and she is responsible for them.

The servant of a man is a guardian of the property of his master, and he is responsible for it. No doubt, every one of you is a shepherd and is responsible for his flock." (Bukhari)

Do you genuinely accept that motherhood is your God-Given role? Say it to yourself and journal it:

"I accept that Allah SWT has blessed me with the honor of becoming a mother, and I'm the guardian of my home and children alhumdulillah."

2. Accept That Motherhood Is Your Purpose

We all have a purpose in life, but sometimes we don't always know what that is. We may think our mission is to be a certain way or accomplish specific goals in life, but that develops more from our wants than our needs.

Sometimes we witness unmarried or childless women dedicate their time to noble acts of charity, alhumdulillah. They run schools, open shelters for orphans, and offer assistance to widows and divorcees because they don't bear the same responsibilities as women with children.

The absence of offspring also enables these women to go out into the world more freely to maintain a hectic job and earn a higher income. It makes what they do seem attractive to a tired stay-at-home mom, as she assumes those women are turning their goals into reality while she isn't.

I used to feel ashamed because I couldn't accomplish certain charitable acts too. I stayed at home to homeschool my six children and felt the burden of their dependence on me. Sometimes this made me feel resentful about motherhood. Once I realized my mission in life was not the same as every other woman, my heart felt tranquil.

Remind yourself that your purpose in life as a parent is essential too, just different. A mother must raise her children into good, wholesome human beings. This may have equal or even greater rewards than other charitable acts, Allahu Alim (Allah only knows).

Accepting that one of the top purposes of your life is to be a mother, will make you feel less burdened and frustrated. Understanding that the responsibility of raising children is not something Allah SWT did to chain you down, but instead as a means of attaining paradise.

Do you accept that motherhood is your purpose? Say it to yourself and journal it:

"I accept that one of my main purposes in life is to be a mother and that this role is vital to society alhumdulillah."

3. Accept That Motherhood Is a Choice

Whether you like to admit it or not, motherhood was a choice you made in life. If you think you didn't have a say in the matter because your pregnancy wasn't planned, know that it was inevitable the day you got married. Why? Because there's no birth control method that's a hundred-percent foolproof other than complete abstinence.

That's impossible after marriage, so the moment you tie the knot, you choose the option of having children. According to the circle of life, the next step after finding a husband is to eventually fall pregnant and raise kids. You may think you have some power to hold off getting pregnant for a while, but the timing and every other aspect of your life have happened by Allah's SWT Qadr (predestination).

Whether you meant to have children early or planned to have them later, if Allah SWT decreed kids for you at a specific time, it was bound to happen. Eventually, you would be where you are, facing the same struggles more or less, and instead of thinking, *"What happened?"* say, *"Alhumdulillah for His blessings."*

When you learn to accept that motherhood is a choice you've made, you'll feel less frustrated with your struggles. This knowledge makes it easier to accept your hardships because your tolerance increases when you think you have a say in the matter. Thus, you're able to bear your responsibilities with the mindset of, *"I'll do what has to be done."*

Do you accept that motherhood is a choice? Say it to yourself and journal it:

"I accept that becoming a mother was a choice I made, and I will bear the responsibility with honor, grace, and dignity, alhumdulillah."

4. Accept That Motherhood Is Going To Be Difficult

Think of everything in your life that means something, and you'll realize it didn't come easy. If it's important, it will have a price attached because that's the way of this duniya (earthly life).

If you're a happily married wife, it wasn't easy to find Mr. Right, and you have to constantly work to keep your relationship thriving. If you're a professional who earned a degree, you studied hard and worked long hours to get that title. If you're a successful entrepreneur who started your business from scratch, you invested money, time, and sweat to reach your goals.

It doesn't end there because nothing worthwhile in life is effortless, and the same applies to motherhood. It isn't easy for a mother to bear children; in fact, it's one of the most challenging feats in life.

When you recount the pains of labor wracking your body or if you've recovered from a c-section, you probably thought there was nothing worse than going through all of that. Then, seeing your newborn's face made you fall deeply in love, and you're willing to go through it all again (well, at least after some time passed).

"And We have enjoined on man (to be good) to his parents: his mother bore him by bearing strain upon strain, and his utter dependence on her lasted two years, show gratitude to Me and to your parents: to Me is (your final) return." (Quran 31:14)

It's tough when your role changes from new wife to new mom, and you face sleepless nights and an aching bosom. Finding free time becomes a gift of the past. Then, your child cracks their first smile or exclaims their first word, and your longings and aches dissipate as you melt.

The day comes when your children become teenagers, and suddenly you're dealing with their mood swings and disrespect. You may think, *"It can't possibly get any worse!"* Then your teen makes salah, and you hear them say dua for you (without being asked), and you know in your heart that your parenting was well worth the effort.

33

I could mention many similar scenarios, but do you see the trend of life? There'll be difficulty with relief, then more difficulty with relief, and that's what we need to accept. Nothing valuable, especially motherhood, will be easy, but knowing that Allah SWT will help us through it, makes all the difference in the world.

> **"For indeed, with hardship (will be) ease."**
> **(Quran 94:5)**

Do you accept that motherhood is going to be difficult? Say it to yourself and journal it:

"I accept that Allah SWT has blessed me with a challenging role but it has immense reward, alhumdulillah."

5. Accept That Motherhood Is Never Done

The frustration of your constant mothering to-do's will gnaw at you and turn into resentment if you think you're supposed to reach a point of saying, *"I'm done."* Accepting that motherhood is not something you add to a list and, "check-off" will help you endure your struggles better.

Motherhood is a never-ending role that changes over time and won't be done until you leave this worldly life. Your children will always need your parenting skills from the time they are born until they get married and become parents themselves.

They might need you for guidance, advice, and as a helping hand in raising their children during challenging moments. Then too, you'll see your kids fumble and show inexperience and want to guide them with your knowledge so they avoid making the mistakes you made.

The sooner you accept that motherhood is not a checklist and parenting will never be over and done with, the sooner you'll learn to embrace your role as a mother as part of your life forever.

> **"Abdullah Ibn Umar saw a Yemeni man performing tawaf (circumambulating the Ka'bah) while carrying his mother on his back. This man said to Abdullah Ibn Umar, 'I am like a tame camel for her! I have carried her more than she carried me. Do you**

think I have paid her back, O Ibn Umar?'
Abdullah Ibn Umar replied, 'No, not even
one contraction!'" (Bukhari)

Do you accept that motherhood is never "done?" Say it to yourself and journal it:

"I accept that Allah SWT has blessed me with this special role of motherhood for a lifetime, and I cherish it alhumdulillah."

6. Accept That Motherhood Is Not About Being Perfect

There is an unrealistic trend of portraying a successful mother as a "superwoman" in today's society. Personally, I denounce using the term "superwoman" or worse, "supermom" because it's demotivating for mothers to think they are expected to be a woman who can do it all, do it all well, and do it all with a smile.

My objection stems from seeing so many mothers obsessed with acclimating to the unnatural ideal of supermom, that it wastes her efforts thinking it's even possible!

Being a wife, running a home, raising children, maybe also working, homeschooling, looking after extended family members, etc., cannot all be done well by one woman. A mother needs support and assistance to do this all successfully.

It isn't even a question of whether she can do the impossible; it's whether she should do the unrealistic. Each mother excels in her way, not in every way, and it's okay to have limits. Accept that trying to be the perfect mom is futile because there isn't one. Only Allah SWT is perfect, and we're merely humans created weak.

"And the human was created weak." (Quran 4:28)

Do you accept that motherhood is not about being perfect? Say it to yourself and journal it:

"I accept that Allah SWT is the Only One Who is perfect, so I should not aim for the unrealistic goal of being a perfect mother alhumdulillah."

7. Accept That Motherhood Is Not an Isolated Incident

Once you graciously accept that motherhood isn't a walk in the park, you'll realize you're not alone in your struggles. I feel overwhelmed every few days, and most mothers go through feelings of distress at some point or another. It's normal to feel overcome by your responsibilities when raising kids, because it's a big job!

An essential step to your peace of mind is remembering that some mothers' situations are more challenging than yours. There are many burdens that Allah SWT did not place on you that other moms have to endure. In Islam, Muslims are advised to look at those below them and not those above them to avoid ingratitude and discontent. The Prophet SAW said:

> "Look at (and compare yourself to) those who are below you, not those above you, for this way; you will not belittle Allah's Bounty on you." (Bukhari)

Another factor to consider is that things are not always what they seem. If you see another mom having a more effortless mothering experience, don't take it as fact.

Everyone is fighting their own battle, and we don't know what happens behind closed doors. T he mother whose life you envy may have other challenges that you would not be equipped to handle.

Like any other major challenge in life, motherhood has its ups and downs. Accept that you are not the only one suffering from your struggles because motherhood is difficult for other moms too, just in different ways.

Do you accept that motherhood is not an isolated struggle? Say it to yourself and journal it:

"I accept that many women are struggling with motherhood too, just in different ways, and our parenting trials are a normal part of life."

8. Accept That Motherhood Makes You Stronger

A good friend once told me that even though being a mom was demanding, she wouldn't be the person she is if she hadn't become a mother. I understood this to mean that she became a better human being overall through her motherhood experiences.

When you reflect on yourself as a parent, you'll see that much of your strength and endurance came from being a mom. Face it, you'd be less resilient and wise, and more self-absorbed and spoilt if you weren't a mother. Raising children builds stamina and selflessness, and if you ponder your life, you'll realize it's the truth!

Think back to who you were before you had kids, and measure how much your physical endurance, emotional stamina, and personal strength have increased. Accept that motherhood made you the tough cookie you are today!

Also, realize how much reward you're earning for the afterlife by your sacrifices as a mother, and rest assured your accumulated points are being banked in the Here-after inshallah. The Prophet SAW said:

"Never a believer is stricken with a discomfort, an illness, an anxiety, a grief or mental worry or even the pricking of a thorn but Allah will expiate his sins on account of his patience." (Bukhari)

Motherhood shows how you can be so much more than the assumption you have of yourself. Before bearing children, you had no idea about the extent of your capabilities or how flexible were your limits.

Accepting that motherhood is strength training to build a better YOU is a sure way to feel more at peace with your tribulations.

Do you accept that motherhood has made you stronger? Say it to yourself and journal it:

"I accept that motherhood made me tougher and strengthened my resolve as a whole alhumdulillah."

9. Accept That Motherhood Is a Trial and Test

There are days when your children will listen and do all their homework and chores. You've completed your tasks on time, and dear hubby says all the right words. Then there are the days when your kids are driving you crazy, you end up fighting with your spouse about petty issues, the house is a mess, and you want to run outside and scream! At these moments, remember dear mom;

"Allah does not burden a soul beyond that it can bear." (Quran 2:286)

This Quranic ayah (verse) has helped me make it through so many tough days when I felt I couldn't endure any more hardships. Reading the verse will help you understand that Allah SWT is the One Who sets your limits and your burdens are manageable.

It may seem difficult to remember during formidable times, but realizing that your tribulations may be a trial will help you endure them. Allah SWT may be testing you so that you can grow as a person or get closer to Him. Realizing this will bring you relief and fortitude.

Learn to accept your motherhood role as a challenge in this world, and know that we're all given different tests to pass. This is necessary to reach the next step towards a blissful eternal afterlife.

> **"And know that your properties and your children are but a trial and that Allah has with Him a great reward." (Quran 8:28)**

Do you accept that motherhood is a trial and a test? Say it to yourself and journal it:

"I accept that Allah SWT may be putting me through trials and tests for my growth and to increase my resilience as a Muslim alhumdulillah."

10. Accept That Motherhood Has Its Rewards

There are two significant types of "payback" for the struggles of motherhood. The first is in the worldly rewards. They are the simple things like hearing your child's laughter, watching your kids grow up wholesome, experiencing their successes, witnessing their faith strengthen etc., and you feel deeply satisfied knowing your sacrifices are worthwhile.

The second reward of motherhood is in the afterlife. It will be the moment when you reap the rewards of your grueling efforts because Allah SWT recognizes the struggles you endured on earth. He invariably knows what you're going through every step of the way. Our Lord gave us trials and tribulations to test us, and parenting is a chance to gain access to higher levels of Paradise.

Can you think of another life struggle as richly rewarding as parenthood?

I'm not sure what's comparable, but whatever comes close, it can't be much easier. Without a doubt, parents will be vastly rewarded for their various sacrifices on the Day of Judgment. We must acknowledge that motherhood has countless blessings and benefits as compensation for long years of hard work and sacrifice.

"Salamah, the wet-nurse of Ibrahim, the son of the Prophet SAW, said, 'O Messenger of Allah. You give tidings of all the good to the men, and you don't give tidings to the women.' The Prophet said, 'Did your female companions induce you to (ask) this?' She said, 'Yes.' He said, 'Will one of you not be pleased that when she is pregnant from her husband, and he is pleased with her that she has a reward like the reward of the one who fasts and prays in the way of Allah? Then when she is in labor, none of the people of the Heavens or the earth know what is hidden for her of (pleasures), soothing to her eyes. And when she delivers, no mouthful of milk flows from her nor a (child's) suck except that she has a reward with every

> mouthful and with every suck. And if (her child) keeps her awake during the night, she has a reward similar to the reward of freeing seventy slaves for the sake of Allah.'"
> (Tabarani)

When we read this Hadith, we can't deny the immense rewards of motherhood. How abundant is Allah SWT in his blessings towards mothers? Every laborious task she bears will have bountiful rewards.

If you set your focus towards this path, you'll find yourself complaining less and feeling more contentment and gratitude. The acceptance of knowing your purpose as a mother is your solace during difficult times.

Do you accept that Allah SWT will reward your nurturing? Say it to yourself and journal it:

"I accept that Allah SWT will reward me abundantly as a mother for all my sacrifices in this world and the next alhumdulillah."

More Ways of Accepting Motherhood

14 SMALLER TIPS TO FIND PEACE

I wanted to add in some additional ways to accept motherhood to remind you that mothering "is what it is" and all part of life. Smile through it, and don't let the small things get you down dear mom.

1. Accept that you may not enjoy a quiet meal or an undisturbed dinner for some time, but remember, your cooking and meal-prepping will nourish your family.

2. Accept that you may not have a full or uninterrupted night's sleep for a long time, but remember, you're raising healthy, righteous servants of Allah SWT.

3. Accept that you may not be the same dress size or even shoe size again, but remember, you're beautiful to the Creator through your deeds and actions.

4. Accept that your house will not be squeaky clean or perfectly organized, but remember, your children will retain happy memories and feel nurtured by a mother who's less focused on the small things.

5. Accept that whenever you pick up the phone to talk to a friend, your child may need something, a cup may break, or sibling rivalry may happen. Remember, one day, your kids will leave home and you'll have the time to make all the phone calls you want inshallah.

6. Accept that you may not have enough time to get ready for appointments and commitments, but remember, you're the driving force behind the future generation's success.

7. Accept that instead of shopping for yourself, you'll probably come home with bags full of necessities for your house and kids. Remember, the afterlife is filled with all the luxuries you wish for and they'll be far grander.

8. Accept that you may drive around in a "mom-mobile" instead of the car of your dreams, and even be referred to as the "soccer mom" or "homeschooling mom." Remember, being a mother is an honorable role that not every woman is blessed with and in Jannah, you'll have all your wishes fulfilled.

9. Accept that others may not refer to you as young and cute anymore, but no one's looks last forever anyway. Remember, your deeds make you beautiful and in Heaven you'll be more unique than the huralayn (the maidens of Paradise known for their beauty).

10. Accept that you may plan and schedule your days to the tee and still have moments that don't go as expected. Remember, Allah SWT is the Best of Planners, and He knows us better than we know ourselves - this is the source of true comfort.

11. Accept that you may not always have complete privacy in your bedroom or even the bathroom with children

around. Remember, be flexible with your little ones and set simple boundaries with your older kids to feel less irritated because it's only for a temporary span of time.

12. Accept that when you finally get a chance to dress up nicely, you can expect to find a stain on your clothes or be unable to find any matching accessories. Remember, these misfortunes make you less selfish and more giving, and they don't really mean anything in the bigger picture.

13. Accept that your phone, laptop, makeup, jewelry, and almost everything you love will probably get used, broken, or lost. Remember, you did similar things to your mom and kids will be kids. Children are not out to intentionally cause their mother distress.

14. Accept that even though life can be crazy at times and full of twists and turns, you'd *never* trade being a mother to your children for anything else, and that's what makes you a great mom!

How To Cope As a Mother

PART TWO

As moms, we wish for days with a quiet retreat of prayer, meditation, and calm. We aspire to read the latest book, listen to inspiring talks, eat healthily, go for walks, and take our vitamins as we should. Ah...the thought, and we can keep dreaming!

The reality of motherhood is far less enticing as our days are more like a haphazard grind as we rush around, herding kids to do this and get that. Packing lunches, stopping sibling rivalry, teaching manners, and reminding everyone to take their belongings while searching for lost homework, books, socks, and shoes.

Yes, moms are the ultimate caretakers of the family; no matter if they're stay-at-home moms or working moms, motherhood is challenging, and there's no way around it.

To your family, there's nothing more comforting than MOMMY when there's sickness or something's hurting. Occasionally, even hubby needs some TLC too! You realize how labor-intensive nurturing can be, and most times, you're so busy taking care of everyone else's needs that you neglect your own.

Motherhood is so much more than a full-time job that's 9-5. Instead, it's a "when you open your eyes to when you close your eyes" kinda job. There's no real time-off for dear mama unless she makes it happen!

When you think of a mother, you imagine someone who's self-sacrificing and nurturing. She's the person who'll ensure that everything and everyone is taken care of. That's all well and good for everyone else, but no one considers whether a mom needs some care and time-out to continue giving.

Therefore, mothers need to ensure that they set specific time aside for themselves. Women must shift their mindsets towards establishing mom-care as natural and vital, so it's at the top of their to-do list.

Alongside this mindset, when a mother deepens her connection with Allah SWT, she learns to release herself from expectations and the need for human appreciation. This will cause her less frustration and resentment in the long term.

Often, a mom doesn't think about her intentions of the efforts she makes for others. She assumes she has to sacrifice constantly because that's what it means to be a nurturer. Most mothers will keep giving, giving, giving, hoping for some worldly appreciation to see them through the grind. But if that worked, parenting and self-help books wouldn't be flying off the shelves.

Finding joy in motherhood stems from having a healthy and balanced mindset. When you rewire your thinking and set your intentions straight, it works wonders in attaining deep contentment.

When you include establishing gratitude to Allah SWT for your countless blessings, it makes you look past your "have nots" to focus on your "haves." This attitude will bring you more barakah and fulfillment, and you'll experience renewed appreciation for your life.

> **"Truly my prayer and my service of sacrifice, my life, and my death are (all) for Allah, the Lord of the Worlds." (Quran 6:162).**

Change Your Mindset!

It Has a Lot To Do With How You Think

Our mindset is directed by our thought processes and beliefs and plays a major role in determining the outcomes of our feelings and actions. Unknowingly, our mindset can make us feel negative, depressed, and anxious, which cause us to lead a more limited life.

The good news is that we can adapt and shift our perspectives to improve our overall well-being, decrease stress, and become more resilient to our motherhood challenges. Here are some ways to change your mindset to become more positive.

Mindset #1: Develop Respect For Yourself

Some moms are so hard on themselves that they can become their own worse enemy! They'll criticize their efforts, feel guilty for not doing enough, reach for unrealistic ideals, and constantly compare themselves. They'll typically only focus on what they're lacking and hardly see to their basic needs.

Changing your mindset to respect yourself as a mom will help you be more confident and attuned to your needs as a woman. You can't do anything well or see to others decently when you put yourself last.

Many mothers think it's selfish to see to their needs when in fact, it's logical. You can't be useful to anyone when you don't feel healthy and happy inside. Even if you do move past this temporarily, you'll struggle to accomplish anything significant and your meager efforts will make you feel frustrated.

Putting your needs first is a principle that you must adopt as a priority. After that, you can improve your other mindsets to encourage more positive thoughts and ensure you become the best version of yourself.

Mindset #2: Develop a Connection To Allah SWT

Never forget that your Creator is the only One Who can truly help you. Not your husband, parents, siblings, best friend, children, or even a therapist. Learn to seek your Lords help first and foremost because He's the One Who makes everything happen.

> **"Call upon Me - I will respond to your invocation." (Quran 40:60)**

When I began to ask Allah SWT for assistance frequently, I felt hopeful more often. I didn't ask for His help in motherhood before, as I would forget or assume I should only call upon Him for major problems.

I would even hold off asking Allah SWT for anything until salah times or on holy nights. Honestly, I didn't realize the power of dua or that our Merciful Lord loves us to ask Him. Since I began supplicating daily, a whole new world of barakah (blessings) has opened up for me.

"I am as my servant expects Me to be, and I am with him when he remembers me. If he thinks of Me, I think of him. If he mentions Me in company, I mention him in an even better company. When he comes closer to Me by a handspan, I come closer to him an arm's length. If he draws closer to Me by an arm's length, I draw closer by a distance of two outstretched arms nearer to him. If my servant comes to Me walking, I go to him running." (Bukhari)

Subhanallah, this Hadith sends shivers down my spine, and I get choked up when I read how much Allah SWT loves His servants. How can you deny this after knowing that when you remember Him, He will remember you? Our Lord is the only One Who can truly assist us in need!

Your life improves when you get into the habit of asking Allah SWT for aid at the first sign of distress instead of asking a person or popping a pill. Your supplications don't have to be only at salah time; they can be while you're standing, sitting, cleaning, thinking, studying, driving, or at any time of the day.

Set your intention to ask our Most Gracious and Most Compassionate Lord to help with your struggles. After all, He is the Best of Helpers, and He loves His servants, especially those who make dua and istighfar (repentance) – all you have to do is ask.

> **"And when My servants ask you, (O Muhammad), concerning Me - indeed I am near. I respond to the invocation of the supplicant when he calls upon Me. So let them respond to Me and believe in Me that they may be guided." (Quran 2:186)**

> **"Verily, Allah loves those who repent and those who purify themselves." (Qur'an 2:222)**

Mindset #3: Develop Your Intention

Why do you try your best to be a wonderful mother each day? Is it to show your husband what a great wife you are, so he falls deeper in love with you? Is it to show your children you're the best caregiver so they'll adore you more? Is it to prove to your relatives and friends that you're an awesome parent?

Maybe you feel that being self-sacrificing is not a choice but a necessity. What comes to mind when you think about why you give so much to others? Is it purely out of love and devotion to your Creator, or does it satisfy a need within yourself?

You hope those you care about the most will appreciate your efforts, even if they don't say it often. But unfortunately, when you don't set your intentions right the first time, your sacrifices happen for worldly reasons. Sooner or later, this ends up being a recipe for resentment and unhappiness.

Why? Because your purpose in life is to please Allah SWT first, pleasing others is secondary and most times not appreciated. This may sound unfair, especially when you're used to relying on instant gratification, but in the long run, you'll feel more content.

People are imperfect and can be pretty ungrateful. So if your sacrifices are for anyone other than the pleasure of your Lord, then expect to experience countless disappointments. Anything sought through the self causes difficulty, while anything sought through your Lord causes ease. This frame of mind is one of my most effective endurance pills.

> **"One who loves for the sake of Allah alone and hates for the sake of Allah alone; and whatever he gives for the sake of Allah alone; and whatever he withholds, withhold for the sake of Allah alone; indeed, he perfects his iman." (Abu Dawud)**

When your intentions are set for your Lord's pleasure and not to please others, you won't leave yourself open to unsatisfying expectations. You don't wait for the pat on the back, the high praises, or any words of thanks. You've overcome the need for self-gratification and understand your rewards are waiting for you in the akhira.

All other forms of gratitude are merely a bonus. Therefore, make your intention fisabilillah (for the pleasure of Allah), and you'll notice a significant difference in the outcome. You'll gain freedom from the shackles of disappointment, find reassurance in your sacrifices, and your drudgeries will seem more manageable.

Mindset #4: Develop Your Gratitude

All of us have gone through demanding days, despair, and desperation at one time or another. Our first instinct is to cry, *"Why me?!"* as we don't realize that sometimes we're being tested, and other times we bring the hardship upon ourselves.

> "Whatever of good reaches you, is from Allah, but whatever of evil befalls you, is from yourself. And We have sent you (O Muhammad saw) as a Messenger to mankind, and Allah is Sufficient as a Witness." (Quran 4:79)

Even when we read the above verse, we're left thinking, *"How unfair is my life"* or *"How unlucky was the hand I was dealt."* We dwell in our woes and feel ingratitude about our lives.

We feel a sense of entitlement because we pray and mostly abstain from bad deeds, which cause us to believe we deserve a free pass from Allah's SWT tests.

If this was the case, why were the Prophets (peace be upon them) put through so many hardships? Why did Allah's SWT most beloved Messenger SAW go through so much tribulation?

That's because our Lord tests us, and He tries us even more as we get closer to Him. When we pray to Him saying, *"O Allah, we put our trust in You, we believe in You, we want to please You"* do we truly mean it?

If so, we should be prepared to be judged on the things we say. If we're not tested, how would we prove our faith and trust in our Lord and not make empty promises?

"Do men think that they will be left alone on saying, 'We believe,' and that they will not be put to the test?" (Quran 29:2)

It's terribly sad to meet mothers who complain a lot, showing a weakness in their iman. I come across these moms often, and it pains me to witness their sense of ingratitude. They don't understand that all the good things they have going for them are not given to everyone.

Of course, I'm not referring to the moms who occasionally vent to their girlfriends or sisters to gain advice and support. I'm referring to those women who constantly complain to anyone who'll listen.

We all know it isn't a good idea to bottle up your frustrations and insecurities, but there are ways to talk about your problems without displeasing Allah SWT and showing a disregard for your blessings.

An Example of Gratitude During Hardship

A sister I used to follow on social media long ago ran an online parenting advice page. She often shared great tips with her readers, and I admired her outlook on motherhood. One day, she mentioned going through a very rough patch.

She shared that she would be taking a break from posting due to the significant hardship she was going through. She expressed her negative feelings but did not complain at all.

What touched me the most about her post was how she expressed sabr and iman during her difficulty. Instead of focusing on herself, she shared her admiration of other mothers who were going through more challenging times than her. She wrote that she still saw so much to be grateful for despite her hardship.

When I last looked up her page, I couldn't find it. However, I'm thankful I had taken a screenshot of the post to ground me whenever I felt ingratitude about my life. Here's an extract of what she wrote (edited):

"I am touched by all the kind words. Do give me some downtime. However, I must say, as much as some of you say you are inspired by my posts, I am actually surrounded by inspiring parents myself. I am also learning from them. Among my friends, too, I have so much to learn. For example:

- *A mother pregnant with her seventh child, while caring for six kids without help, one of them special needs, and carrying out her homemaker duties.*

- *A mother of five with a child who's recovered from cancer and carrying on with her dawah, teaching, and business duties.*

- *A mother with autistic children gave up her career to care for them.*

- *A single mother who started a business to support her child.*

- *A mother of four raises another four children from her husband's other wife, thus raising eight kids and holding two jobs to support them.*

- *A mother who raises ten kids into huffaz and even finds a second wife for her husband because she's too busy with the kids.*

- *A mother who was pregnant with her sixth child, only to find her husband has secretly got a second wife and that wife is pregnant too, and makes peace with her.*

- *A mother in a wheelchair who works to support her three children.*

- *A mother with five kids and one special needs kid, and still teaching and did her Masters.*

- *Mothers whose children have returned to Him SWT and still are going through life after their initial grief.*

I have many more examples of real-life mothers whom I know personally and are really awesome, mashallah. Behind these mothers is Allah SWT, and they are all my inspiration, and I am nothing compared to these mothers. May Allah help us and guide us, and please forgive me if I need some downtime for a while. May Allah bless you for your encouragement." – Umm Anissa.

Alhumdulillah, in her hardship, she remembered to look to those around her who were in greater difficulty and found hope during her bleak time. She was grateful for not being in a worse situation and found solace in dealing with her lesser struggle.

Those are real-life situations that happen everyday and all over the world. If we open our eyes and really look, we'll see the blessings all around us. Allah SWT doesn't give us more than we can bear, and His generosity and mercy are plentiful; we simply need to start taking note of them.

When I read about the struggles of those mothers, I couldn't fathom going through even half the burdens they encountered. My life hasn't been easy, but I've learned to appreciate all I have, and see my hardships as minor and effortless compared to theirs.

My Big Tip For Gratitude

I encourage mothers to get a shukr (thankful) or barakah (blessings) journal to write in daily. When you face moments of forgetfulness, try writing down everything you're grateful for in your life. Set it as a recurring habit, as this reinforcing behavior will make you realize what you've got going.

When life is tough, open your journal and read all the blessings you wrote down before. This will remind you to be grateful when you're not feeling positive about your motherhood life – call it your anecdote in times of dismay.

I do this very thing, and it's one of the reasons I published journals specifically for Muslims. You can get both the *Shukr Journal* and *Barakah Journal* at *muslimsjournal.com,* or use any notebook to start your gratitude journey.

Mindset #5: Develop Your Thankfulness

Last but not least, look at your life and think, *"Would I change it or be without my kids?"* Your answer will be *"No way!"* This was the life Allah SWT chose for you. You were meant to be born in this time, this country, this body, this situation, and have this family.

Don't question the Qadr of Allah SWT and embrace the fact that He gave you this destiny. It's the part of life we don't have a choice in, just like how we have no say in our appearance or who our parents are. That's beyond our comprehension, and we appreciate what we have compared to what we could have received.

When you start noticing your blessings by observing someone who has a more challenging life than you (there's always someone), it will guarantee to keep you grateful. This has worked like a charm for me.

Also, be thankful for what you went through as it got you to where you are now. It took grit and determination to get this far, so without a doubt, you *can* see it through till the end.

Lose It, Don't Use It!

11 Things a Mother Needs To Lose To Feel Less Weary & Stressed-Out

L osing certain negative traits will help you become a happier mother and, in turn, give you greater fulfillment. Sometimes, looking at yourself from another person's perspective can give you an idea of which actions may be causing you additional strain and anxiety. Let's look at some unfavorable qualities mothers should lose if they want to flourish.

1. Lose Your Anger

Being a parent, having mom friends, and observing other women outside, there's no denying that many mothers have become crabby. A lot of us are struggling with anger issues, and I used to wondered why.

I discovered the leading causes of agitation are increased stress levels and high expectations placed upon moms in a fast-paced society. An annoyed mother fails to realize that her irritation causes her to feel even more stress, which is bad for her overall health.

Mothers should learn to stop overreacting to every little thing their child does and "chill-out" a bit. In the past, I too, had to make a concerted effort to change my grumpy attitude as a mom. I made the conscious effort to stop snapping at my kids, criticizing and yelling at them over insignificant things.

In Islam, we're taught to talk to our children as we want them to speak to us. They're watching us constantly and will mimic what we say and do. They'll adopt many of our mannerisms and etiquette, if not when they're young, then later as teens and adults.

Thus, controlling your anger is not only good for your well-being as a woman, but teaches your kids to be less inclined to give in to their anger.

2. *Lose Your Pride*

Open your heart to your husband or a good friend and lose the "woman pride." Express your hardship to someone you trust and besides feeling better, you'll feel relief at having a shoulder to cry on. The Prophet SAW said,

**"No one who has an atom's weight of pride
in his heart will enter Paradise." (Muslim)**

Don't feel like a failure when you express your limits as a mother, since we are insan (mankind), with many weaknesses. Admitting your vulnerabilities is a sign of strength and shows that you know your place in the world and you're humbled by Allah's SWT power over you and everything around.

73

Talking to a trustworthy girlfriend is an excellent idea if you want a comforting, empathetic person to give you wise advice. If you want sympathy from your husband, it's best to ask him by saying something like, *"Honey, I don't need you to fix anything; I just need a hug and to tell me things will be okay."*

Your spouse will take the hint that you simply need re-assurance and not the usual male problem-solving talk that can sometimes make you feel worse.

3. Lose Your Guilt

Most of the time, mothers are burdened with a guilt complex, and never feel they do enough or think they are nurturing effectively. Not one of my family members or friends has ever said the words, *"Alhumdulillah, I am a great parent."* or *"Mashallah, I did enough for my kids today, so I'm going to take a break."* Can you think of any mom who would even admit that aloud?

Mothers seem to sell themselves short and constantly need to compensate for what they feel is lacking. This causes them pressure, and if they're a helicopter parent as well, they raise kids who lack self-sufficiency which places a greater burden on them. What helps when you feel the guilt coming along is to keep a record of what you do.

Think of your day and write down all that you've accomplished for your family and how you maintained your home. You'll feel surprised by how much things you list each day, and your guilt will diminish instantly.

Guilt is also the shaytaan's way of keeping you focused on failures, so you lose hope and give up the struggle of being a good believer and parent. Know his game and realize your worth! I cover more about mom guilt in part three of this book.

4. Lose Your Control

Do you notice how controlling you can be as a woman? Mothers want things done a certain way and almost always think they can do everything better. Sometimes they assume they can do it even better than hubby can!

To be fair, not all moms are like this, but I've noticed a majority are extremely controlling, and some are major control freaks. These moms want their kids to wear the blue sweater instead of the red one, take a lunch box instead of a lunch bag, and eat this type of food instead of that type.

Some moms go too far and imagine they're the ones preventing their family from the world's downfalls. They think their protectiveness and safety measures keep all harm at bay for their husband and kids. When there are no mishaps that day, they believe it's because they're doing a great job.

Besides being prideful astaghfirullah, it's a lot of pressure for any mom to bear!

When a mom relinquishes control and remembers that *nothing*, especially the safety of her family, is in her hands, she'll feel the burdens lighten from her shoulders. Sure, you have to tie your camel to ensure your child doesn't run loose in traffic, but that's a logical part of caring.

Change what you *can* control and accept what you *can't*, then leave the rest to Allah SWT. This is the motto I've developed. We take precautions, but realize that we're not the ones ultimately in control of anything.

You'll feel enlightened and empowered when you think of things this way.

5. Lose Your Self-Doubt

How many women do you know who openly claim to be good mothers? I don't know one. It's not common to see moms pat themselves on the back for a job well done. Instead, you'll hear them say things like, *"I don't think my efforts are working"* or *"Maybe I need to change what I'm doing"* or *"I could do so much better!"* The list goes on.

Many moms suffer from significant self-doubt. Even without comparing themselves to other women, they formulate ideas borne out of high expectations and lofty ideals. Adding in the comparison factor, it gets out of hand, and their self-doubt can eventually turn into depression.

The key is to trust yourself and your abilities as a mother by listening to your gut. If you need more convincing, ask your kids, *"Am I a good mom?"* Unless you're the "Wicked Witch of the West," your kids will always believe you're the best mom ever!

In most cases, even your husband will agree you're a great mom if you ask him. It's just YOU who doesn't think so because of your constant self-doubt. So ask yourself, *"Where did I get this guilt complex from?"* Once you know the answer, squash the thought like the annoyance that it is!

6. Lose Your Comparison

This one's big as it's such a female trait to compare oneself to other women. For example, when you visit a friend's home, you pick up on the interaction with her children, how well-kept and nicely decorated her home is, what she cooks, wears, looks like, and who she's married to.

You instantly feel inadequate and that you don't have it "all together" like that mother. You mistakenly assume she's doing a better job than you, and forget your self–worth. How ridiculous does this sound when you put it into perspective?

Often, the mothers you compare yourself to aren't better than you. They may happen to excel in one area while you excel in another. That woman is making an effort to appear worthy in front of her guest; it's not her everyday reality! You're so focused on her capabilities that you fail to see her shortcomings.

It's okay to pick up valuable ideas and habits from other mothers (especially if they're more experienced than you). But don't make the trivial things they do bigger than it is and instead, focus on extracting from them the things that will improve your life.

I used to feel like I fell short when I saw other moms give their kids homemade organic foods. It's something I wished I could do for my six kids. But when I looked at my situation and analyzed it as a whole, I realized I couldn't possibly do that *all the time.*

I looked at the mom I was comparing myself to and realized that she had less children than me and didn't homeschool them. I felt relaxed when I looked at the bigger picture. We can't be good at everything, but we *can* be skilled in our own way.

7. Lose The "Yes Mom" Mentality

As a woman, you don't need to say yes to everything asked of you. You have a beautiful heart if you love to help and assist others, but you can't keep it up all the time. It's also not possible to be everything to your family and everyone else.

If you stretch yourself too thin, you won't have the patience and energy you need to take care of yourself, your immediate family, home, studies, work, etc. Everything will come crashing down sooner or later, and you'll do nothing well.

Many people perceive stay-at-home-moms (SAHM) as more available than working moms. They assume SAHM should take time to help the community, and as a result, these women are pressured to volunteer more than others.

For example, at one point, I was a working mom in a stressful and time-consuming job. At other times, I was solely a stay-at-home mom. During another period, I homeschooled my six kids in various grades. Out of all those responsibilities, I found working a stressful job easier in many ways.

It was less demanding to go to work because I came into a clean environment, got breaks, had time for lunch, and my kids weren't asking me a question every five minutes. I always had assistance and support from my employer and co-workers. So, as you can tell, I know first-hand that being a SAHM is not more manageable in the least!

Circling back to the "yes-mom" mentality, I know it won't be easy to avoid saying yes to people when you want to say no, but here's one way to do it. Don't ever say yes to anyone on the spot when they ask you to commit to something.

Instead, say you need to check your calendar or ask your husband. Tell them you'll get back to them via a text message. This keeps you from making irrational decisions on the spot that you'll regret later, and not feel embarrassed if you need to say no.

If the person is pushy and wants you to answer immediately, realize they're in the wrong. In this case, you should be more determined to answer *"no"* because they're not thinking of your well-being.

Once you've considered the time commitment to their request and made sure it doesn't overlap your obligations, make an informed decision. Remember, every minute of your day doesn't need to be filled with work and commitments; you also need time to unwind and reflect.

If you decide to decline a request, don't feel an iota of guilt or give a long list of reasons why you can't do something. Only YOU know what's best for yourself as a mother, and not the other person. If you feel you need to give an excuse because that's just how you are or you care a lot about the person who's asking, simply say, *"Sorry, I can't this time, maybe next time inshallah if I'm able."*

Saying no to loved ones will be way more difficult, but you must set boundaries even with them. For extended family and very close friends, I do what I can to help. Whenever I can't, I offer to help them from my home, which is usually easier than simply saying no.

As for husband and kids, when I can't fulfill their requests, I'm honest with them and explain that they need to respect my limits if they don't like to see me irritable and stressed out. It will seem tricky at first, but it gets easier the more you do it and when others gets used to you doing it. Always know, you have the right to decline commitments and shouldn't feel guilty for not taking on everything.

An Example of a Mom Who Knows What's Important

I have a friend who has many kids and is hardly involved with anything outside her home. I used to think she was selfish for shutting herself off from community commitments, barely maintaining friendships, and not volunteering for events.

I was the opposite. I did all of these things and was popular among people. Guess who came out on top? She did. I got burnt out many times, and my family had to sacrifice due to my absence. When I began to set boundaries, some of my girlfriends didn't like me so much. I learned a hard lesson in life and began to look at that friend in a new light.

From the beginning, she knew her limits and set boundaries (of course, this fluctuates according to how much responsibilities you have). My friend has a lot on her plate, so once she put her family's needs first, she realized there wasn't much time for anyone else. She wasn't selfish; she was just a smart woman who respected her limitations.

Nowadays, I've adopted her limits and I'm much happier with my life. I do what I can when I can, and I always put myself, my husband, and my kids first. After that, I give my time to extended family and close friends and perform charitable acts to the community for the sake of Allah SWT – all within my boundaries.

Remember, everyone loves a "doer" and the "social butterfly," but from my experience, those women don't show a healthy balance in all areas of their life. Many I know have unhealthy eating habits, weight and stress issues, or act like grumpy, frustrated wives and mothers.

It's not easy to find a healthy balance in every aspect of your life, because being a dedicated Muslima, wife, and mother is no leisurely walk in the park. However, it can be done with the correct mentality.

8. *Lose Your Insecurities*

I can't count the times I was asked, *"What do you do?"* and I shyly responded, *"Oh, I'm just a stay-at-home mom"* or *"Well, I just homeschool my kids."* I'd then brace myself for the judgmental response, *"Is that all you do?"* because many women are the worst cheerleaders of traditional roles.

There were a lot of times I thought, *"Why do I diminish what I do?"* I wouldn't mention to others that I run multiple online platforms or volunteer hours of my time helping wives and mothers who struggle in their daily lives.

I felt that if I wasn't making a decent income or pursuing something society deemed "successful," it didn't count. I was embarrassed for not working a "regular job" like the other moms I met, and assumed they were criticizing my choice behind my back.

In reality, the blame was my fault. Some women are ashamed to be "just mothers" and are afraid to proudly say, *"Yes, I work as a full-time mother from home al-*

humdulillah. "It's truly a full-time job to be a good wife, mom, and homemaker. In fact, it's above and beyond full-time, and nowadays, I say it with conviction.

Mothers don't count their efforts as beneficial compared to employees. That's why, when we're asked to spare some of our time, we feel guilty and say, *"Sure, no problem, what time is good for you?"* because you think, *"Hey, it's just me, the stay at home mom, my plate is full, but you can heap on more because I have no boundaries."*

Why do women undermine the acts of charity they do for their husbands, children, and homes? They forget that it's a constant act of charity to be a dedicated wife, mother, cook, cleaner, and all-around homemaker. It's not less valuable than giving a sum of money to feed the poor or volunteering at a shelter for the homeless, so let's ponder why we value these good deeds more?

9. Lose Your Codependency

Do you know what it means to be codependent? I urge you to look up the symptoms and see if you have some of those traits. I've noticed that many women have this crippling habit, and it's the leading cause of their exhaustion and worn-out state. To avoid being long-winded, here's a quick summary of the signs of codependency.

Codependents feed off others' neediness and devote all their energy to their loved ones and friends. They allow another person to define their mood, happiness, and identity. Some additional signs include:

- Difficulty making decisions in relationships.

- Difficulty identifying feelings.

- Difficulty communicating in relationships.

- Valuing the approval of others more than their own.

- A lack of trust in yourself and having poor self-esteem.

- Fears of abandonment or an obsessive need for approval.

- Having an unhealthy dependence on relationships, even at your own cost.

- Possess an exaggerated sense of responsibility for the actions of others.

If these signs ring true in any way, you may have a habit of overextending to others and not being true to yourself. Begin by losing the mentality of thinking you have to solve everyone's problems and be constantly producing something. *Supermom to the rescue* is not considered a virtue; it's exhausting!

When I realized this about my personality, I began shouldering some responsibilities off my plate and onto my husband and kids. For example, I ask my husband for help but don't tell him how to help me. If my child gets a cut on their finger, I kiss it and send them to their big sister to put ointment and a bandaid on. I say, *"Please ask your smart brother if you need something fixed"* or *"Ask your sweet sister to help you get a snack."*

I offer appreciation to my husband for his help and give compliments, treats, and privileges to my older kids for assisting me with the younger ones. It teaches children to be responsible, the older ones love feeling useful, and you having fewer headaches to deal with!

As a woman, you know your husband and children's strengths and weaknesses, so use that knowledge to assign tasks to them. They might even do the job better than you! Save yourself a lot of pressure and stop being "Ms. Know–It–All" and "Ms. Do–It–All."

10. Lose Your Ideals

Women tend to want things done a certain way and at certain times. My hand is raised because I'm guilty of this too! A mother who wants to feel less exhausted needs to sometimes take a step back. The saying, *"If you want something done right, do it yourself"* is true, but what's the outcome of following this ideal? Burnt–out mommy!

So what if your hubby gave the kids cereal for dinner? Your older child put the dishes in cupboard A instead of cupboard B, and the other kids won't hang their clothes, preferring to "lay them" on the closet shelves. So what? All this stuff is not as important as the people we love.

Close your eyes, take a deep breath and say, *"Oh Allah SWT give me the knowledge to focus on what really matters."* When you feel the need to have things done your way, realize how unimportant those things are and don't sweat the small stuff.

Have fun with your family and stop worrying about what needs to be done all the time. Relax and enjoy being a happy wife to your hubby and joyful mom to your amazing kids. Say alhumdulillah to your Lord for your beautiful family and abundant blessings.

11. Lose Your Impatience

I almost didn't mention patience as a virtue because most people believe being a mom means you already have patience. Also, as a mother, you're likely tired of hearing, *"Be patient"* as it can grate on your nerves! I felt it deserved a mention because nowadays, patience is not the standard of every mother.

Say what?

Besides having more pressure these days, women who live in modern societies have become far more impatient than the mothers of the past. We live in a world of instant gratification, and as a result, displaying sabr has become less common. Of course, this is not only prevalent among mothers but most people in society.

We want our kids to learn to read by five, write paragraphs by seven, and memorize the Quran before high school. We find it difficult to set aside a couple of years to breastfeed or take time off from work to raise our young kids.

We expect our children to understand what we require and listen the first time we say something. We've forgotten that our little ones learn so much from trial-and-error, and there's really no rush to educate them faster than the kids before.

We've evolved, but our kids are still just kids!

Our expectations have become demanding, but the blame is not solely on moms. Society has set these high expectations that mothers in the past didn't have to deal with. An example of this would be worrying about non-GMO foods, which has placed a lot of pressure and guilt on parents.

In Islam, having sabr is a virtue. I speak from experience when I tell you that the more I learned to be a patient woman, the more everything fell into place. I've experienced so much goodness that came from me being comfortable with waiting, over being hasty.

Previously, I was quite an impatient person, made many mistakes, and "worked harder not smarter" due to this fault. It was a major source of stress for me as a wife and mother, so if you have this trait, learn to overcome it to find greater relief.

Set It, Don't Forget It!

10 Traits To Help a Mother Cope Better & Feel Less Exhausted

Setting healthy boundaries and expectations dictates how people can treat you, how they can behave around you, and what they can expect from you. Your limits are drawn from the framework of your core beliefs, perspectives, opinions, and values, and they are constructed from your life experiences and social environments. Let's look at some positive attributes you should establish if you want to succeed in your mother-hood role.

1. Set Your Limits

I have an internal clock that knows when I've spent too many hours with my kids. Too many days over my limit, and I feel like I'm going crazy! I know I need adults to talk with and frequent breaks.

Sometimes, I'll simply head to my bedroom for some moments of peace or call a friend for a chat. I will go through a drive-thru to grab a hot chocolate or read a book at the library if I need to get out and clear my head. Whatever it takes to unwind your thoughts – do it! A rested mom who knows her limits is a happy mama!

Mothers have ambitions too. If I ponder two of my major goals, it would be to study Islam with scholars and travel the world with my family. However, that's not possible in my current position as a parent of six dependent kids. Following your dreams because you can and realizing the consequences if you do, is what it comes down to.

Sure, I could start some studies or suggest to my spouse that we take a trip nearby, but I rather wait and write my goals on my "would-love-to-do" list. This list can be attained after the responsibilities to my young children, because I *choose* to wait a few years until they're less dependent on me. In the meantime, my husband and I can plan and save for both our goals to become a reality someday inshallah.

As a mom, I'd also love to feed my kids all organic foods and hearty home-cooked meals every single day. What happens is sometimes we eat sandwiches, have frozen vegetables instead of fresh, or end up eating food bought from outside. We all have our ideals, but there has to be limits on what you can do during the moment you're currently in.

When I feel guilty for not being the best parent due to circumstances, I make a dua such as, *"Oh Allah the Most Great, You know my every thought and intention, so please let us derive benefit from this food."*

If you ask, I genuinely believe Allah SWT can make the food you can afford, be as nutritious as the expensive organic foods. Because He's the One ultimately in charge, not us, and He can make anything possible if we can't do more. Our Lord knows our intentions, so we do the best we can and leave the rest to Him – that's having iman!

As a mother, you want to do the ultimate best for your family, but if that causes you hardship or financial strain, leave it for later. Try to do better when you have more time, money, or your kids are older. Just be realistic and know your limits, or you'll become overwhelmed.

2. Set Your Boundaries

Sometimes it's easier to say no to our immediate family than to our extended family, friends, and even strangers! As women, we feel we must take on the world to prove that we can do it all instead of settling to be a "mere mother."

Sadly, if you think like this, you are insulting yourself. I believe wholeheartedly that the role of a mother is like a badge of honor because of the endurance you need and the stamina it takes to keep it all together.

Setting mental boundaries for yourself is one way to say, *"I can do this, but I choose not to do this"* because you know it will cause you strain. Instilling boundaries with the people in your life is crucial to your well-being and to cope. It helps you determine who can ask for what and when, and whether you can add it to your list or not.

There's no need to feel like others won't like you because of your boundaries. Honestly, people admire a woman who isn't a doormat and takes care of herself. They'll look up to her as an example and want to learn from her.

We can help people in many ways that don't cause us difficulty, like through our dua, comforting words, and compassionate support. This is significant and people who know about the power of supplication will appreciate this wholeheartedly.

I often cannot physically help someone in need because it is a hardship for me and my family. Remember, your well-being takes priority over another person's needs, and don't confuse this with being uncaring and selfish. There are ways to help someone without putting yourself out.

I've done charitable acts like ordering a delivery meal for a family who had a baby instead of cooking the meal myself and transporting it to them. I've shipped friends flowers and chocolates when they were going through a hard time, and checked on others via text and voice messages when they felt isolated and needed a sympathetic ear.

I've also arranged with a group of sisters to pitch-in money for a housekeeper when someone in the community was ill and needed cleaning help. I'm sure you've heard of those women's groups which assist new moms with a rotating meal plan for the family. If you're part of those kind of groups, you can even send groceries or pizza for the family without having to cook it yourself.

I'd personally prefer any of the above assistance compared to a woman taking time to come to my house (which may be a long drive) and dropping off a meal she had to cook while seeing to her responsibilities. I would feel less guilty knowing I wasn't putting pressure on another busy mother.

More people would help more if they didn't feel pressured to do time-consuming acts out of guilt. I get so fed-up at the expectations placed on us by silly traditions and sensitive feelings. Admittedly, I also hold mothers accountable for not setting realistic boundaries for themselves, judging other moms harshly, and caring too much what people think.

3. Set Your Communication

Mothers often expect their husbands and children to read their minds or notice their body language. Yeah, right, dream on. Most men and young kids are not great at female intuition, much to our detriment and frustration. But that's just the way it is and fortunately, we can change the outcome, and here's how.

Women have to learn to communicate better!

Go to your husband and discuss your feelings, but please tread cautiously. Do not accuse or blame him for the problems you face. Instead, tell him how you feel by saying something like, *"Honey, I'm feeling exhausted lately."*

When you express to your spouse a problem, be prepared for him to jump in and try to problem-solve your issues (that's a man's nature). If you want sympathy, ask for it and stop expecting him to be a mind-reader.

Communicating your feelings to your husband is a big part of your relationship. Remember, it's his children and home too. You don't need to solve every issue alone, and he won't deny it if he's a decent man. I believe most men are good husbands and fathers but we don't give them the chance to help us in their own way.

If you cannot verbally solve your problems with dear hubby, write him a text or email to get your point across. But please, I urge you to always be respectful, kind, and not attack him by your frustrations.

The same applies to your kids. Don't expect them to know what you require. Ask for help and remember they are immature and inexperienced beings. If they have a ton of homework, don't let them guilt you into thinking they can't do their chores as well.

When I explain to my children that I am one person who is seeing to eight people's needs and can't do it alone, they are much more accommodating. Keep your speech short, stick to the point, and be real with them, and they'll be more motivated to help.

Many women need to also lose their passive-aggressive nagging and start communicating better about what they really want. Aim towards being direct in speech but in a kind tone and without aggression. Start teaching your family to hear you by using clear directives and simply expressing your expectations and needs.

Don't play word games, manipulate, and expect those around you to guess what you require. And also, don't moan and groan as this makes people stop listening to what you have to say which will make you feel more annoyed.

4. Set Your Spoiling

There are days when you're exhausted, have a pounding headache, aching shoulders, and you desperately need some peace and quiet ASAP. Most mothers will simply suck it up and bear their pain with resentment.

If your husband or child came to you with similar ailments, you'd become a mother hen. You'd most probably rub away their aches and pain, serve them something comforting, and send them off to rest. That's typical of the empathetic nature of a mother, and it's what makes her one-of-a-kind.

But when is it your turn to be cared for?

Do you ever ask your family for some spoiling? Don't hold your breath if you're waiting for them to offer.

Once again, no one can read your mind, and hardly anyone will offer to spoil you voluntarily. It's laughable just thinking about it! So, how do you get some spoiling too?

It's simple, just ask for it and take any and all offers.

This is not the time to show pride; this is your body telling you it has needs and a right over you. You must listen to it because your body hurts for a reason, and you are not a martyr. Remember, no one admires the sacrificial lamb, maybe just you.

When I sincerely ask for assistance and explain how I need the help, my husband and kids are keen to please. They will bring me painkillers, rub essential oil on my temples, or massage my tense shoulders. I will even get a mug of herbal tea or a warm meal if I ask.

I allow my spouse and children to spoil me just as I spoil them. It also makes them feel good to help and know exactly what I want. In return, I don't become resentful like those grumpy ol' moms who lament that no one cares when they're unwell.

If I didn't set some spoiling for myself, I would never receive it from others. My family isn't more caring than everyone else's; I simply set the expectations and made them happen by asking for what I need.

5. Set Your Sense Humor

Do you notice how serious you become as you get older and deal with parent life? I used to laugh a lot before motherhood and I was the girl who'd giggle at any joke, no matter how silly it was.

I saw the humor in everything because I never took life too seriously. This all changed after I had children, and the constant responsibilities of nurturing wore me out and made life seem a lot less funny.

I'm sure you can relate!

After each child, my burdens grew, and I became more solemn that, at one point, my husband claimed I'd become a bit of a drag. Of course, I was annoyed he said that, but I knew he was right if I was being completely honest.

I remember one day, I saw my hubby and kids laughing at something, and it actually irritated me! I stopped myself from saying something negative when I realized they were just having fun, and my annoyance was directed at myself. I had become so bogged down by my duties that I had become the drag my family thought I was.

From that day on, I decided to return to the girl I used to be and take life less seriously. Okay, realistically, it isn't possible to be the same person you were in your youth because you didn't have ten percent of the responsibilities you have now. Also, it isn't easy to be carefree and not allow life to overtake your humorous side, but you can still be a mature version of your younger self.

I noticed how much I had missed laughing, and as a result, I now have a collection of humorous quotes on my Pinterest boards and several funny videos saved to my YouTube account. I also share them sometimes with my husband, girlfriends, relatives, and older kids for a shared laugh.

So dear mom, find what makes you laugh and stop letting your responsibilities make you boring. They're never-ending and you're the only one missing out on the fun that life has to offer. Enjoy the precious moments with your husband and kids as the time with our loved ones is limited and will be over before we know it.

6. Set Your Needs

Setting your needs as a woman and a mom is crucial to gaining success. Self-respect will allow you to practice mom-care because you'll believe you deserve it. If you don't understand how to appreciate your worth, how do you expect others to appreciate you?

Just as your husband and kids have needs, so do you. Your needs are not only limited to shelter, food, clothing, and transportation, but other things like regular doctor and dental visits, exercise, healthy foods, comfortable apparel, etc.

How can the queen of the house look and feel worse than everyone else?

When you give yourself the respect you deserve, you'll feel more like the mistress of the house and less like a slave to it. Respect your role as a mother and realize that you have an important place in the family and society. Never short-change yourself!

I know it doesn't come easy, so make a conscious effort to take care of yourself on a daily basis. A lack of self-respect can result in self-destructive behaviors like stress-eating and online addiction. How you feel about yourself dramatically affects your willpower.

If you respect your needs, you'll care for yourself the way you should. In turn, you'll also be able to set boundaries in your life and relationships. You won't allow people to treat you poorly, and if they do, you'll recognize your worth and walk away from them.

Others will not be able to influence your opinions or negatively disturb your mental peace and stability. I'm sure you can judge how much you've allowed this to get out of hand, but fortunately, you can change old habits.

7. Set Your Path To Taqwa

I cannot emphasize enough the importance of having taqwa. Taqwa means to have true faith and belief in your Lord, and this God-consciousness is the lifeline to keeping your sanity as a woman.

Taqwa brings about a state of vigilance in avoiding any action that would earn the displeasure of Almighty Allah. It also diminishes the love of this world and controls materialism, pride, envy, ingratitude, or any weaknesses we struggle with.

As a result, the more taqwa we have, the more we're protected from falling prey to our nafs (ego). Many dissatisfied mothers allow their emotions to control them and overlook their blessings. You instantly become more satisfied with your life when you have strong faith, and develop gratitude and sabr as was discussed before.

You don't allow the small stuff to get to you and avoid complaining about the things you don't have or can't control. You'll also realize your life could be a lot harder, and that you've been saved from enduring a worse situation.

A way to uplift your taqwa is to focus on strengthening your bond with Allah SWT. You can do this by ensuring that you regularly maintain your salah and implement prayers like tahajjud, haja, and istikhara to help you during your tough moments (you can find explanations of these prayers on my website).

You can also instill dua, dhikr, Quranic recitation (by your favorite qari), watch a scholar on YouTube, read books of Hadith and seerah, or attend a halaqa with like-minded sisters. All these acts can increase your faith, so you can deal with the challenges of motherhood and regain more fortitude and endurance.

8. Set Up Your Mom Care

I've spoken about taking care of yourself as a woman numerous times, but I want to ingrain it in your mind because it's truly important. Setting aside mom-care is not optional; it's a necessity!

Any effort you put into mom-care also has huge payoffs for your family. When you "fill your own cup" you have more patience and energy to pour out to others. If you need some mom-care ideas, here are some I suggest:

- Practice being compassionate and kind towards yourself to renew your energy.

- Pray and supplicate to your Lord often.

- Journal to release your pent-up emotions.

- Turn on calming tunes or nature sounds.

- Do stretching exercises.

- Write in diary, type a blog article, or work on writing an ebook.

- Read a motivational book or listen to an audiobook.

- Watch an educational YouTube video or a TV series you enjoy.

- Chat or text with a girlfriend who motivates you.

- Make yourself a delicious cool drink, hot cup of tea, or mug of yummy cocoa.

- Go out for a salad, to the library, or browse your favorite store.

- Go for a walk in nature.

- Design a quote on your computer, print it, and hang it up to uplift you.

- Avoid social media and chat groups till you're feeling mentally strong.

- Make a cozy spot for yourself to think and meditate.

- Write down everything weighing you down, stressing or bothering you to avoid overthinking and worrying.

- Set a date or go on an outing with you spouse, child, or a friend.

- Chat with a loved one or book mentoring with a coach if you need advice about a challenging situation.

- Download a calming app or a cute game on your phone to zone out.

- Do some charitable acts for others to focus less on yourself.

- Practice breathing deeply and make dhikr.

- Organize a small area of your home or tidy something that's been bothering you.

- Declutter some of your stuff online or on your phone to feel less digitally cluttered.

- Simply sit on the couch, put up your feet, and close your eyes.

- Take a nap or relax on your bed.

- Analyze your stress to know what caused it and how to avoid more of it.

- Paint your nails, do a pedicure, put on a face mask, or have a bubble bath.

- Think of three things you're grateful for and say alhumdulillah for them.

- Look at photos on your phone of good times, and when your kids were young.

- Hug your husband and children tightly.

- Cut out something from your schedule that will cause you relief.

- Choose something tasty to eat in moderation, so you receive the joy without the guilt.

9. Set Your Sights On Long-Term

I've noticed that as women, we tend to think short-term and live in the "now" more than men. Making decisions in this frame of mind is a cause of exhaustion and over-whelm.

So many times, mothers come to me for coaching and complain about their difficulty with a particular situation. Sometimes, I merely suggest they realize how their struggle is short-term, and their challenging stage will be over before they know it. This is another aspect of sabr that I discussed previously.

A perfect example of short-term thinking would be when a mother feels despondent about her last trimester of pregnancy being tiring or her newborn won't stop crying from colic. When you're going through these situations, it feels traumatic and never-ending.

On the other hand, when you look at your troubles in a long-term point of view, you realize that most problems are a temporary hardships. With this in mind, you're more prone to set aside time for your difficulty; understanding that you need to go through this for the greater good and for a short period of sacrifice.

This mindset will allow you to have more endurance, so you won't feel helpless and hopeless about your challenges. As the saying goes, *"Short-term thinking is for suckers."*

10. Set Your Expectations

Remember, your kids are young and don't have a fully developed prefrontal cortex. The prefrontal cortex is the part of the brain that controls our rational thinking and judgment. Knowing and understanding how the mind of a child works, opens the door to a wiser way of dealing with them.

As a woman, you think, feel, and react differently than a man does. Therefore, how well you understand your husband, sons, and men in general, will help you communicate better with them. When we realize that we can't judge others based on our thought processes, our expectations change dramatically.

Often, we mistakenly assume what those around us are thinking and feeling. We can't understand the choices they make or why they act a certain way. Many mothers suffer with this frustration and don't see that their lack of understanding is causing their agitation.

When I began to analyze my children's brain development, as well as how men's thought processes worked, a whole new world of insight opened for me, alhumdulillah. Due to this revelation, I highly recommend that women take the time to learn about child and male psychology. In this way, you'll know what to expect from your family and not assume their efforts are less productive than yours.

How To Thrive As a Mother

PART THREE

One day I discovered I didn't know who I was anymore. I looked at my reflection and saw a Muslima, a wife, a mother, and an educator, but I didn't see who I was as an individual. I realized that I had neglected the person I used to be, and worse, I didn't even know what I enjoyed doing anymore.

Unfortunately, this is the sad state of many women when they forget how to balance their lives. Mothers get so caught up seeing to everyone else's needs that they forget their own and lose themselves in their responsibilities.

After many years, they discover a certain emptiness inside and wonder who they are. These feelings usually surface when your kids get older, they go off to college, or become independent and not need your nurturing as much.

Now I'm not suggesting you do anything drastic because motherhood is vital and necessary to the family and society. Moms have an enormous responsibility to rear the fathers and mothers of the future generations, and if we do this right, our reward is abundant and everlasting.

Parenting is a constant grind and can overtake your life if you let it, but there are ways to make it less overwhelming and more enjoyable. As we know, anything worth achieving requires determination, grit, commitment, and endurance. Aiming to find a balance as a mom without a doubt won't be easy, but the fruit of your labor will be worthwhile in the end.

There's no harm in having an independent mission as a woman if you know how to do it smartly. You don't need to give up who you are or what you enjoy doing, and you mustn't neglect your health and the little things you love. Like everybody else, a mother has the right to have the time to be someone with goals and ambitions.

Before we dive into the heart of this book, it's crucial to analyze your state of mind. This analysis will give you an indication of your likes, dislikes, wants, and needs. I use this process with some of my clients, and it's always shocking to find that they struggle to answer simple questions about themselves.

Often, they will need to contemplate for some time to figure out their wants and desires. It sounds ludicrous, but I can't judge these women for being disconnected from themselves. You see, I too, was in a similar situation many years ago. I thought I knew myself well, but soon realized I only remembered the young girl I used to be.

In reality, that girl did not have the exact wants and needs as the woman I became after motherhood. This realization was staggering and showed me that I no longer had a clue who I was as I matured. This is the reason I created questions that are absolutely necessary for a mom to know herself and learn who she really is (okay, at least somewhat).

Get To Know Yourself

YOU THINK YOU DO, BUT YOU ACTUALLY DON'T

Only YOU are the expert of your inner workings. You are in charge of your thoughts, emotions, and actions. Your personality is shaped by your upbringing, self-awareness, and principals. By knowing who you are and what you want out of life, it can give you a strong sense of self-worth and confidence in your abilities. In this chapter, I share some ways you can get to know yourself and why it's important.

1. Discover Yourself

I'd like to walk you through a process of discovery I've used to help myself and others. I urge you to try it and see where your mindset lies. Grab a pen and paper and answer these critical questions about yourself. You can find the questions at the end of this category and also use your *TMM Reflection Journal.*

My list of suggested questions is what every woman should ask herself, especially if she doesn't have a clue what she wants to do. Find a quiet place to read them thoroughly and write your answers truthfully. Ask Al-lah SWT for guidance and start with bismillah for more barakah.

1. What do I enjoy doing?

This is something that brings you joy, and you look for-ward to doing it. It's a thing that you derive pleasure from and could even be a passion you wish to pursue. It's not something that makes you feel stressed out, tired, or burdened. For me this passion is writing.

2. What would I like to achieve?

This can be anything, such as learning the deen, studying the Arabic language, or taking up cooking, cycling, hiking, calligraphy, or gardening. It can even be as small as committing to a coffee date with a friend twice a month or having a weekly facial. It's something on your mind to achieve, but you've put it on the back-burner.

3. What are my hobbies?

These are things you like to do for fun or you did before you had kids and want to continue doing. It can be something that you'd love to accomplish in your spare time for self-enrichment. Some examples include reading, cooking, scrapbooking, sewing, crocheting, crafting, painting, playing an instrument, or taking up a sport.

4. What are my goals?

These are ambitions you want to achieve, both short-term and long-term, and they are goals you hope to accomplish in your lifetime. A few examples include learning another language, writing a children's book, studying fiqh (Islamic understanding), taking a natural remedies course, etc.

5. What am I good at?

This should be anything you're good at, and don't be shy to acknowledge your strengths. It could be creating handmade crafts to sell online, homeopathy, business, technology, nursing, teaching, writing, volunteering, etc. These are things you're passionate about and already have some talent.

6. What am I able to do now?

Depending on how busy you are at this point in your life, try to pick at least one thing you could make time for. Then, commit to sticking to it for a specific time frame. For example, you could attend a weekly halaqa, pursue a freelance career from home, volunteer monthly at a charity, or study part-time in the evenings when your kids are asleep.

You could get a coach to brainstorm your ideas over a virtual meeting, go to the gym in the early hours before the hustle, or even write short articles for a blog. Don't let this cause you more strain though, remember you're still a busy parent; it's just not your only pastime.

7. What are the benefits of doing this?

This is the benefit you'll derive from engaging with your hobbies and goals. For example, will you increase your knowledge of deen, earn enough money to buy something big, get some time away from your responsibilities to keep your sanity, keep your mind sharp, get fit, or just be a better person emotionally and spiritually. Everything you do in life should have a beneficial purpose; otherwise it isn't worth the time.

Take your time making these lists, as it's pretty eye-opening to realize how deep you'll need to think about what you enjoy doing. You may realize you've forgotten yourself for so long that you must discover what kind of person you are again. When you try it, I assure you – you'll feel an increase in self-worth and enjoy your role as a parent, thanks to your newfound balance.

If you think of the mothers you know from past generations, how many of them achieved their dreams? Sadly, many of them didn't. Being a mom is not an excuse to become a nobody who doesn't make time for herself. You don't need to only be consumed by your home and family - you can have a life too!

Get some help and lose the guilt! You are a person with wants, needs, likes, and dislikes, and you can still be a good wife and mother at the same time. So make your intention, say bismillah, ask Allah SWT for guidance, and pursue some dreams!

Let's Recap The Questions For Self-Reflection

1. What do I enjoy doing?

2. What do I want to achieve?

3. What are my hobbies?

4. What are my goals?

5. What am I good at?

6. What am I able to do realistically right now?

7. What are the benefits of doing this?

2. Assess Yourself

Take some quiet time to think about your life from another person's perspective. Observe your situation as if you're looking in and critiquing yourself. Start by pinpointing the problems you see and do your best to keep an unbiased view of your situation. Get a sheet of paper and pen, or use the *TMM Reflection Journal.*

Follow These Steps:

1. Draw three columns and title them with the headings, *Problems, Solutions,* and *Resolutions.*

2. Now, write down every problem you can think of in the *Problems* column.

3. Brainstorm solutions to these problems and write them in the *Solutions* column.

4. If you can't find solutions for your problems, write them in the *Resolutions* column, and scratch them off the *Problems* column.

5. The problems in the *Resolutions* column are usually the cause of your immense frustration and hopelessness.

6. To solve the problems in the *Resolutions* column, you'll need someone you trust to intervene and guide you. It could be your spouse, a family member, close friend, mentor, or someone in your local community who's knowledgeable in Islam and free of cultural bias.

3. Enlighten Yourself

Take time to read about the great women in Islam and their struggles so you don't feel that your suffering is a punishment or unfair.

Reading the story of Asiya R.A, who was married to Firoun and raised Prophet Musa A.S, made me appreciate my husband and see our arguments as petty. Asiya R.A endured being married to a tyrant who tortured and killed her horrifically. She kept her faith strong and was wise enough to know that her reward was not in this world but the afterlife.

When I hear stories of the disobedient children of Prophet Adam A.S, Prophet Yaqub A.S, and Prophet Nuh A.S, I feel somewhat reassured. I realized that having issues with my kids does not always mean I'm doing something wrong as, at times, our children are a trial for us.

The Prophets (peace be upon them) were honorable and great men, yet some had challenging children. Thus, the fault may not lie in our failure as parents only, but can also be a test. Allah SWT says:

> "Do the people think that they will be left to say, 'We believe,' and they will not be tried? But We have certainly tried those before them, and Allah will surely make evident those who are truthful, and He will surely make evident those who are false." (Quran 29:2-3)

Listen to scholarly talks and educate yourself regarding the reward for women who are promised paradise. Our beloved Messenger SAW said,

> "When a woman observes the five times
> of prayer, fasts during Ramadan preserves
> her chastity and obeys her husband; she
> may enter by any of the gates of Paradise
> she wishes." (Tirmidhi)

Believing women are promised gifts beyond our imagination and will live in everlasting bliss. You'll find relief in your hardships by focusing on this during the tough days.

Educate yourself on women's rights in Islam and know what's required of you and what's fabricated by culture and tradition. In this way, you won't feel guilty about not implementing silly cultural burdens.

Remember, the Prophet's SAW daughter Fatima R.A would do housework until her hands hurt, but she was reminded of having faith and the virtue of steadfastness. This story has helped me look at my life as incomparable to the hardships faced by more noble women.

> "Fatima went to the Prophet complaining
> about the bad effect of the stone hand–mill
> on her hand. She heard that the Prophet

had received a few slave girls. But (when she came there) she did not find him, so she mentioned her problem to Aisha. When the Prophet came, Aisha informed him about that. Ali added, 'So the Prophet came to us when we had gone to bed. We wanted to get up (on his arrival) but he said, 'Stay where you are.' Then he came and sat between me and her and I felt the coldness of his feet on my abdomen. He said, 'Shall I direct you to something better than what you have requested? When you go to bed say Sub-hanallah thirty-three times, Alhamdulil-lah thirty three times, and Allahu Akbar thirty four times, for that is better for you than a servant'" (Bukhari)

Next, you can write your answers to the questions below on a sheet of paper, or use your TMM Reflection Journal.

Questions For Self-Reflection

1. What are the traits of some great women in Islam?

2. What traits do I already have like them?

3. What traits would I like to acquire from them?

4. *Analyze Yourself*

I've always been interested in psychological evaluations and personality tests, perhaps due to my Psychology major. I love to understand people's behavior and what makes them tick.

When I was a young girl, I wanted to know everyone's star signs, not the weekly predictions of course, just how people born in the same month share similar traits. However, I let go of that when I learned it was not Islamic.

I've found a better way of analyzing people's character traits through online personality tests. I've also heard certain scholars mention that taking some of these tests is good for learning about your character as well.

I've used the *Enneagram* and the *Myers-Briggs Type Indicator (MBTI)* tests. The latter is the more popular of the two. The Enneagram test helps you find your specific personality type among the nine Enneagram types. It's common to find a little of yourself in all nine types, but one of them will stand out as being closest to your nature.

The Myers–Briggs Type Indicator test is a 93-question assessment that places people into one of 16 personality types, each with its own strengths and weaknesses. It's based on Carl Jung's original theory that humans experience life using four psychological functions - sensation, intuition, feeling, and thinking. Some Fortune 500 companies use this test during their recruitment process.

You can find either of these tests online if you're interested in taking them. I think it's beneficial to get to know yourself and what makes you tick when you don't have a clue. I found it helpful to pinpoint my strengths and weaknesses, especially since I was someone who used to be very disconnected from myself due to how I was raised.

I want to caution you regarding the dark side of personality evaluations though, as it can make some people put themselves in a box and fail to grow. I knew two women who were deep into analyzing themselves and would use it as an excuse and say, *"Well, I'm just this kind of person, and people have to accept me for who I am."*

They had defined themselves as empaths and became consumed with embodying their character trait. They came across as ultra-sensitive and unique, and told those around them to treat them with kid gloves.

However, the irony was that they were brash and down-right mean to others, so I guess it was a one-sided empathy. Their bubble-wrap mentality also made them believe that only fellow empaths could understand them. It become highly irritating for "non-empaths" to be in their company.

At one stage, my eldest daughter began taking personality tests of her own accord and became a bit obsessive. I had to remind her that at the end of the day, we are individuals and shouldn't place ourselves into categories like a robot.

We must take these tests with a pinch of salt as Allah SWT created us unique and special. No two human fingerprints are identical, not even the fingerprints on our two hands look similar; that's how different we are, subhanallah! So use these personality tests as a guide to kickstart the *get-to-know-yourself* process and move on from there.

Let Go of The Dreaded Mom Guilt

Before we start looking at principles of surviving motherhood, I want to focus a little on the crippling trait of mom guilt. If you deal with this type of guilt, and have it as bad as some women I've met, it's holding you back in a big way.

Let me tell you a story about my only sister

My youngest sister is a wonderful wife to her husband and an awesome mother to her three young boys.
She's maintained a successful career for over ten years,
earned a marketing and human resource degree, and
passed with the highest final grade in the continent alhumdulillah. She did all this while juggling being a Muslima, wife, mom, sister, and friend.

She runs a methodical home and cooks delicious and
healthy meals for her family. She exercises a few times
a week and is on a healthy eating plan to stay fit and
trim. She takes her vitamins most days, has a skincare
regiment, and dresses simple, modest, and smart.

She contributes to the family's financial budget, owns
her car, and hosts occasional dinner parties and family
get-togethers with ease. She's also an amazing mother
who doesn't cut corners due to her busyness, and is a
practicing Muslim who always keeps up with her fards.

Now you may be just like her, or you may be thinking
to yourself, *"Oh wow! She sounds amazing."* There's
just one problem...she doesn't think she does enough! At
the time, my sister didn't think she was thriving as a
woman and a mom. And when I told her she was truly

doing so much in her life, she said, *"Yes, but I don't think I'm doing anything well."*

I was shocked by her confession.

So I asked her, *"Are you seeing to your children's well-being? Are they happy and thriving? Is your husband unhappy or agitated? Is your home tidy, somewhat organized, and mostly clean? Is your salary decent, your work manageable, and your company satisfied with your progress? Didn't you earn a degree while juggling being a wife, mom, sister, friend, employee? Are you not a believer who is staying away from evil and implementing your fards?"* She answered, *"I guess so."* Then she sighed and said, *"I guess as moms we'll always have guilt no matter what we're doing or where we are in life."*

That's when I knew I had to share this chapter with other mothers. You see, just as I judged my sister's insecurities because I felt she was shouldering her responsibilities superbly, I, too, had done the same thing for many years unfortunately.

So I'm going to fess-up too. I'm a mom-guilt survivor.

And you know what I've learned from my 20+ years of being a mom? My guilt complex did nothing good for me, only loads of bad. The guilt held me back and chipped away at my self-confidence. It didn't allow me to be more successful, make my husband and kids happier, or enable me to have a thriving home life.

As women, we must ask ourselves, *"Why do we bear so much guilt? Where does it stem from?"* Mom guilt only breeds negative thoughts like doubt, anxiety, and uncertainty. It's more prevalent in new, working, single, and overwhelmed moms but does affect experienced mothers in some ways too.

As moms, we've been blessed with the unique talent of being kind, nurturing, and empathetic to others, but relentlessly hard on ourselves. A significant amount of mom guilt manifests when we compare ourselves and ask endless questions like: *"Are my kids watching too much TV? Do I look fat? Am I losing my looks? Should we be eating organic food? Shouldn't my kids be learning that? Am I a bad mom for giving my kids pizza twice this week? Why can't I do what that mom is doing?"*

In today's times, we're being pulled in various directions during a 24-hour day. We flit between home, work, school, appointments, extracurricular activities, you name it. The mothers of today have extra burdens on their plates that our mothers and those who came before didn't have to deal with.

We've fallen into this frame of mind, feeling the need to entertain our kids and keep them happy *all the time.* We also have the extra burden of comparison through social media and smartphones, so it's no surprise that we feel outshined by everyone around us.

I've found these factors to be leading triggers of mom guilt.

There's no such thing as the perfect mom. Heck, there's no such thing as a supermom, because no one can do absolutely everything on her own in a 100% manner. This kind of introspective self-critique is very common in females. In fact, men tend to report lower rates of depression and other mental health problems than women.

I truly wish more women would come to terms with the fact that motherhood is a life-changing experience. Kids come with an entire host of demands, concerns, pleasures, responsibilities, and emotions. Your focus shifts to your child's wellbeing, but it's essential to remember that you can't give what you do not possess.

So How Do We Beat Mom Guilt?

What do we tell ourselves to overcome mom-guilt? We must believe in our abilities and focus on what we can realistically do in our situation as mothers. Firstly, trust your intuition and understand that worrying never resolves anything. Instead, do a brain dump and get all your worried thoughts out of your head and into an actionable format.

Once you've written down all your worries, do a little research to find solutions to your problems, but don't dive too deep into trying to solve them fast. Push yourself to move forward with what you feel is right for you and your family, because if you overthink it, you'll become overwhelmed and do nothing (I did this too many times to count).

You can also write down the activities scheduled in your day to include even the most mundane things like, eat breakfast, brush kids teeth, drive kids to school, etc. Once everything is on recorded on paper, identify where schedules combine, time overlaps, and windows of freedom occur.

Simply put, you cannot do *everything* for *everyone* all the time. Trying to do this is a recipe for disaster! Don't fall into the same trap over and over due to your unrealistic expectations that end up making you feel hopeless.

You can even write some motivation on sticky notes and place it somewhere you look at often. Perhaps something like *"Life happens and it's okay to not be awesome all the time"* or *"I'll do my best and make dua for the rest."*

Understand that there'll be days where you'll buy fast food and the laundry won't be done. Accept that parenting life has ongoing chores until your kids leave the nest and maybe even beyond.

Your home won't be tidy for long and that's fine because you can't live for potential house guests and need a place to feel at ease. Your kids will always need you for something so make peace with not having quiet unless they're busy.

There'll be days when you feel as if the weight of the world is on your shoulders, but in those times, maintain your self-respect and understand you need time-off. Be kind and forgiving with yourself, and don't bring yourself down, but accept encouragement and support. You can also hire help if need be.

As a mother, you are an adult with young lives depending on you. Your necessities must be met for you to function at an optimal level. You'll need sleep to nourish your body and spend extra time nurturing your relationships, faith, and connection to the community.

Satisfying even your simplest needs adds to your strength as a woman which in turn strengthens your household. So schedule that morning stretching session, take time to eat a nutritious breakfast, and don't neglect your check ups, haircuts, or a simple task like getting comfortable shoes.

As a mom, you're a vital part of the family so don't feel a single ounce of guilt for taking care of your needs first.

Make Your Health a Priority or You'll Pay Dearly

I t was at the end of 2017 where I became sick a lot. At first, I developed an eye infection on my right eye which made the entire side of my face swollen and extremely painful. That lasted for two weeks and it took another week for my face to look somewhat normal again.

Soon after that, I developed viral pneumonia which lasted for three weeks. It was so bad that I had a fever and chills for one week and terrible body aches that were only relieved when I fell asleep. Then I developed a cough that lasted another week and I tried every home remedy under the sun but it was a stubborn bugger of a sickness!

This wasn't how I usually experienced being sick in my adult life and I wasn't sure if my immune system was weakening or the strains were getting worse. To top it off, something more weird happened.

After finally recovering from pneumonia, my son took me out one evening for a seafood dinner. As we left the restaurant, I started to slowly go into anaphylactic shock! It seems I had mysteriously developed an allergic reaction to shellfish overnight. I had enjoyed crustaceans all my life without issues and thought, *"Oh my God, this is becoming ridiculous!"*

Alhumdulillah, I didn't have much of an appetite since being ill because if I'd eaten my usual portion, I would have needed an ambulance to take me to the hospital. People later told me that a shellfish allergy is pretty dangerous, and before this incident, I had no idea what it meant to experience anaphylactic shock.

Only by Allah's SWT mercy was I prevented from eating more that day because I got severe symptoms after consuming a small portion. I recall how my body broke out in hives, I experiences painful abdominal cramps, severe back pain, unbearable itching at the craziest places, body chills, coughing, and swelling of my throat where I could hardly breathe.

I remember the day with such clarity because my symptoms occurred while driving home from the restaurant with my young son in the pouring rain. Not only was it difficult to see the road ahead, but I had no idea what was going on with me. I kept thinking, *"I need to get my son home safely without making an accident."*

When I reached home, I collapsed on the living room floor in a heap of pain, begging Allah SWT to grant me relief from the pain. My husband and kids were concerned and didn't know what was happening as I could hardly speak or explain my condition.

I rushed into the shower hoping the steam would open my passageway and relieve me of the intense itching. Eventually, I collapsed in bed in a fetal position, profusely praying and moaning in agony feeling confused about my state of health. My husband wanted to take me to the

ER, but I refused as I couldn't imagine moving another inch and finally fell asleep for hours.

I know this is a dramatic story, but I wanted to share it because it has many lessons to learn for mothers. I had to reflect on why I went through one thing after another and faced these outlandish sicknesses that I hadn't experienced before. Then, it dawned on me.

I believe my immune system was weak because I'd recently gone through some extremely traumatic experiences. I was also dealing with many toxic people in my life who were hurting me deeply, but I was too much of a pushover to break free.

You see, I thought self-care meant exercising, taking baths, and thinking of my physical needs. I hadn't realized that I'd allowed myself to be trampled on by friends and had no boundaries with even my loved ones. I was such a doormat that it began affecting my health! That day, I knew I needed to make some dramatic changes, or I'd become a very sickly woman.

After much research and studies on women's health, I've concluded that we can make ourselves sick or contract diseases from a stressful life. Bad health doesn't only stem from what we eat or lack of exercise, but also from our mental and emotional turmoil. Being a healthy person is not a choice; it's a necessity!

So please mom, don't put off your health needs until tomorrow, take care of yourself now, or you'll pay dearly as I did...or worse.

My 3 Steps Towards Better Health

As mothers, we tend to put ourselves last when it comes to our health. Bad eating habits, lack of exercise and too much stress can make us feel lethargic and get brain fog. If your body isn't getting the right nourishment and enough rest, your energy levels will be low, your mind won't be alert, and it will take you longer to complete your tasks.

With lack of time as a constant deterrent, I try to incorporate as much healthy steps as I can manage to boost my well-being so I'm able to keep up with wife and mom life. Here are three ways you can start being more healthy if you've neglected this area.

1. Cut Out The Bad

For me, a big part of getting healthy was to cut out sugar and processed foods as much as possible. This stopped my food cravings and made me feel less hungry. At first, you think it will be difficult, and there's no way you can live without your sweets and fries, but it's possible when your mind is in the right place.

I learned to eat more mindfully and less emotional when I realized that binges and cravings are largely related to our feelings. What helps me the most is meal planning and substituting the foods I love to make it work. In the long run, it helps me feel good about myself for having self-control, which results in mental, physical, and emotional health.

There will be days when you can't eat mindfully, you're too stressed to care, and the need for instant gratification trumps your better judgment – I've been there and sometimes still fall into this. On those days, be kind to yourself and just get back on the wagon as soon as possible.

Some days will be too overwhelming to keep to a plan and you need all your willpower to keep your head above water. Don't give up entirely because you had a couple of cheat days. If you mainly keep to your good eating habits, those few weak moments won't matter as much.

What has never worked for me is to go cold turkey off everything I loved and almost "punish" myself for eating sugar and junk food. Even if you start eating half the week better, it will be an improvement over eating mindlessly every day. Keep your goals small and realistic as the kinder you are to yourself, the more you'll respect yourself and eventually not want to put unhealthy foods in your body as a choice.

I still a struggle to eat optimal all the time, but I know it's due to my hectic life with six kids, so I do the best I can and get back into my healthy habits more often than not. As I mentioned, stress is a significant factor in eating unhealthy foods; therefore, you must reduce your stress before eating better.

You can start this by:

- Cutting down on your commitments if your life is too busy.

- Taking off responsibilities that are not your duty.

- Avoiding toxic people who drain your time and energy.

- Not saying yes to everyone and over-committing yourself.

- Suppressing feeling guilty for not being a certain way.

2. Put In The Good

Drink water often. I know you've heard this a hundred times before, but here's the thing, it's life-changing! I used to put this off because I forgot or didn't have time. But if you're determined and tell yourself you need to be healthy for everyone's sake, it's amazing how you find the time.

I purchased a few large, metal, quality water bottles and set two in my bedroom near my bed and desk, one in my living room, and another in the kitchen. I made sure to drink from it before mealtimes, tea breaks, and salah times, thus attaching a new habit to an old one. I felt less hungry and lethargic, I looked better, and my mind was crystal clear. I've heard that adding a tiny bit of Himalayan pink salt helps retain water in our body better, so I do that as well.

Eating enough protein is another way to help you feel full and not binge on junk food. Eggs are easy to prepare as deviled, scrambled, or as an omelet. Add some sardines, turkey, chicken, and lots of green vegetables to make it super healthy and filling.

If you dread making healthy meals, keep it simple because making elaborate meals and snacks can be overwhelming and you won't stick to your plan. Try making a sandwich and load it with salad, refrigerate cut-up fruit and veggies in a container that's ready to munch. Eat nuts and seeds on the run as a snack, so you don't get tempted by fast food, have dried fruit when you're out of fresh fruit, or have a bowl of oatmeal as a filler.

I've found that the quickest way to get my daily intake of fruit and vegetables is to have a smoothie. Here's my recipe for an energy-boosting, healthy, quick meal. To make a single serving, in a blender, liquidize:

- 1 banana

- 1 cup blueberries (or other berries)

- 2 tsp plain greek yogurt

- 1 cup filtered water

- 1 cup frozen kale (or spinach)

- 4 slices of beets (unsweetened from a can is fine)

- 1/2 stalk of celery

- 1 tbsp honey (optional for sweetness)

To ensure that I'm always able to make a smoothie, I freeze a few bananas and use frozen berries in a bag. I prefer blueberries because they're a superfood with high antioxidants. To make your smoothie more nutritious, you can also add a tbsp of probiotic, flaxseed, and collagen powder (read about the benefits of these powders).

Many smoothie recipes are online, and others are loaded with different supplements full of vitamins. Find the best recipe for your needs and see how easy it is to get your boost for the day. I feel energetic and satisfied after I've had one of these, and it's a great meal replacement too. Also, don't forget to take your daily vitamins, as I see the benefit from this habit.

With every change, start simple, so you have a higher chance of sticking to it. Please note that these tips worked for me, but you should always research healthy tips that are suitable for your body type and needs. Make time for your health mom; it's not a luxury but a super necessity to be a healthier woman.

3. Keep Fit and Meditate

I try to exercise at least three times a week. When my children were young, I'd walk in the park while pushing them in a stroller. Now I have a mini trampoline in my bedroom, and I'll rebound to get in my steps when I can't get to the gym. Research the benefits of rebounding to see what a fantastic and easy exercise this is. Mom life is no walk in the park; the only way to survive it is to be fit and healthy.

However, I know that many moms find exercise to be ultra boring. Try to put on some beats and dance in your bedroom for exercise, or try belly dancing which is not too difficult, super fun, and hubby will love it! Those are some exercises I did when I was a younger mom, but now I keep it low impact and add in some strength training using light weights, resistance bands, and a balancing ball

As for your spiritual and emotional health, instill some quiet time to maintain your sanity and take frequent breaks during the day to unwind. Your well-being should be considered a need and not a "do-it-if-I-get-time" afterthought.

You can do things like:

- Meditate after salah for a few minutes, thinking of Allah SWT and His creation.

- Make 10-20 dhikr after salah or while cleaning and cooking to bring you calm.

- Do stretches in the morning or before bed to loosen your tension.

- Say your morning and evening duas with deep contemplation to ask for relief.

- Play Quran in the background while you work.

Taking time to be a woman and not only a homemaker and nurturer gives you the energy to carry on week by week and the freshness to do things well. Plus, good health is priceless and isn't guaranteed, so don't neglect it. The Prophet SAW said:

"Take advantage of five before five: your youth before your old age, your health before your illness, your riches before your poverty, your free time before your work, and your life before your death." (Albani)

Enjoy Motherhood & Overcome Overwhelm

50 Tips To Help You Thrive

O ur daily motherhood stress is not only caused by our environment but also by ourselves. Take a look at your life and analyze who is affecting you and what's all on your plate, and it will shine a light on your situation.

It's important to note that many of us were not given the ideal parenting skills from our parents or society. We were thrown into the role of wife and mother as if we already knew how to do it with ease. Some of us overcame this eventually and dubbed it our "newfound knowledge," whereas others still continuously struggle.

It would have been nice to know what to expect and have taken a wifehood and motherhood course before heading into these life-changing roles. Think how prepared we would have been and the decisions we would have made with the knowledge beforehand.

To combat this in some way, I decided to put together fifty motherhood tips gathered from my twenty plus years of parenting experience. I hope these tips will help if you're struggling in motherhood due to needing help being organized and structured, feeling motivated, and understanding your personal setbacks. Let's go!

Tip #1 Wake Up Earlier Than Everyone Else

When I rise earlier than my family, I find time to pray, supplicate, and meditate. I also enjoy a hot cup of tea or coffee while planning my schedule. When I sleep in, I don't have the same opportunity to do any of this, and I won't feel quite as relaxed or prepared for the day ahead.

However, I also do what my body needs by noticing how my emotions and energy levels fluctuate. For example, on certain days, like when I'm on my hayd (period), I allow my body to rest and choose to sleep in (plus, I don't need to rise early for fajr). Once my kids are awake, it's full steam ahead, so I need all the sleep I can get to deal with the chaos since I'm not at my peak. Though, most days I rise early and it's usually when I'm the most productive.

Tip #2 Write Down Everything & Categorize It

I write it all down, and I mean *anything* and *everything* I need to do daily. All moms should adopt this process, commonly called a "brain dump." It feels like you're clearing your mind and transferring the mess in your head onto a page. This visual extraction of your thoughts is a form of decluttering your mind.

After you write everything down in your *Brain Dump* list, add what's important to a *Master To-Do* list. This is an extensive list of your critical to-do's. Once complete, you can further divide your to-do's into *Mini-To-Do* lists. These mini lists should be categorized with relevant labels. For example, my *Master To-Do* list has the following *Mini To-Do* list headings:

Master To-Do List:

- Calls/Emails/Texts

- Online & Paperwork

- Home & Family

- Outside

The *Calls/Emails/Texts* list is for anything I need to do pertaining to correspondence. The *Online & Paperwork* list is for things I need to do that requires going online or dealing with mail, forms, and legal documents. The *Home & Family* list is for anything I need to do for my household, hubby, and kids. The *Outside* list is for any errands or appointments I need to set or attend.

If you need further help, I've designed a personal planner with all this laid out, which you can find on my website at *zakeeyaali.com*. Alternatively, you can write your list on a page or turn to your *TMM Reflection Journal*.

Tip #3 Prioritize Your Duties To Avoid Overwhelm

As mothers, we want to do it all, but realistically we can't. You need to define your most important priorities and determine how you spend your time. That's where prioritizing your to-do list helps. After you create your *Master-To-Do* list with sub-categories, divide your items into specific labels. I use tags like:

- Extremely Important

- Somewhat Important

- Less Important

For example, let's assume you have an infant and a toddler, plus you wish to pursue an Arabic language course. You could put your little ones needs and your studies under the category of *Very Important*, but this may cause issues. You'll soon realize that even though studying might seem important, you may not get to do it because you're overwhelmed by your children's demands.

A smarter option would be to add your Arabic studies under the *Somewhat Important* label because you can wait on studying, but can't put your infant's teething or your child's tantrums on hold. If there's one thing I've learned as a mom of six kids, when your kids need attention, they'll distract you any way they can, and often through negative means. This is why I suggest that moms of infants and toddlers shouldn't take on anything hectic, and realize their young kids dependance is temporary.

Under your *Very Important* list should be a list of the priorities you need to fulfill. Your *Somewhat Important* list is also a priority, but it's not time-sensitive. Your *Less Important* list is what you hope to accomplish someday (but isn't a big deal if you never get around to it).

From my experience of mentoring many mothers who felt burnt-out and overwhelmed, I recommended that they commit to being full-time moms if they have kids under three. Motherhood is hectic, and if you add studying or a career to the mix, you must accept that you'll feel more stressed-out and will need to make certain concessions.

Tip #4 Become Organized Even If You Don't Enjoy It

Even if you hate organizing or aren't the type, start becoming organized. Once you see the difference that organization makes in your life, you'll never look back. Organizing doesn't have to be extreme; do it in the simplest and most balanced way.

Start by sorting out yourself, then your home, kids, and surroundings. It's one of the best ways to save time, get on track, and feel like you're at the top of your game. As I mentioned in tip #1, start by making lists for everything and anything on your mind.

Next, write or print out lists for you and everyone in your household who has a stake in what's being done (even your helper). Depending on age, you can make lists for your kids and add columns, stickers, and pictures. These can then be hung on the fridge or a central wall space and even placed in a home binder. I highly suggest creating meal plans and cleaning lists as well.

If you add all of this to a home binder, you can place it at a convenient location for easy access. What exactly is a home binder, you wonder? It's a file with index tabs inside a ring binder containing your printed lists.

I've designed a printable template with all the included add-ons, which you can find on my website at *zakeeya ali.com*. The categories I title in my home binder are:

- Chore Lists (for each child)

- Weekly Meal Planning Lists

- Cleaning Lists

- Honey–Do List (my hubby prefers this to being nagged)

Tip #5 Implement Routines & Structure

After you make your lists, set up a daily structure. This is achieved by creating routines for yourself, your home, and your kids. An advantage of establishing routines is that it enables you to speak less and have your children take some responsibility off your shoulders.

Making use of simple guidelines that are easy to understand leaves no room for miscommunication and error. The *what, why, and where* are thus covered by your initial lists. Routines transition into habits, which make it easier for you to implement defined structures over time.

It's absolutely vital to hold everyone accountable for their responsibilities in order to cope. This includes holding yourself in check as well, and keeping your kids on task with consequences and rewards.

Tip #6 Time Your Tasks

Set a timer to do specific tasks because our perception of time is often unrealistic. For example, say you intend to wipe a spill on your fridge shelf but end up cleaning the entire fridge. This in turn causes you to be late in cooking dinner and a snowball effect occurs.

Your kids start to whine and get mischievous from being hungry which heighten your stress level and makes you feel irritated. Hubby comes home from work and asks, *"What's for dinner?"* and gets a glare from you because he should've guessed what you're going through.

By sticking to a set time per task, this scenario is unlikely to happen. You'll avoid taking on too much at one time and your timer will remind you to do a task only in the amount of time allocated. This method also works great when you're surfing the web.

For example, I'll set a timer when I go on specific sites that I know can be distracting. Pinterest and Youtube are two of the biggest culprits. I'll scroll through these sites for a set amount of time, and force myself to stop when my ringer goes off. I give myself about 10–30 mins to surf, then close my laptop until I have another spare moment to browse.

Tip #7 Bookmark & Use Sticky Notes

To avoid getting distracted while browsing online, I use the tagging function on my devices. The bookmark option on your web browser and smartphone is a great tool to save a page for later perusal. I bookmark interesting sites that I want to read when I have more time, and also text myself important links and notes.

Using sticky notes is another helpful way to set reminders and to delegate tasks. My eldest daughter taught me the benefits of using these notes and it's been such a lifesaver. For example, you can use sticky notes to write "leftovers" on storage containers with the date to avoid food spoiling.

You can also place sticky notes around your house to reinforce rules for your kids. It even helps you stay on track as you can stick reminders and to-do's that are crucial to remember. As a bonus, it serves as handwritten love notes for hubby and kids in their lunch bags!

Tip #8 Remain Consistent In What You Do

This point is crucial and I wish it was emphasized more to us as kids. I've realized that to be successful at anything in life, the key is to remain consistent. Many of our failures stem from not following through with what we decide to do, and inaction becomes our most significant handicap. When I saw this weakness in myself, it prevented me from blaming others or my situation when things didn't work out.

Lack of consistency is also a big reason parents struggle with disciplining their children. They don't remain consistent with rules and punishments, so their kids continue pushing their buttons. When kids see inconsistency with consequences, they misbehave. So my advice is to select one area of your life to improve and remain consistent in doing it before moving on to the next thing, and see what a difference it makes!

Tip #9 Declutter Your Stuff

If something doesn't have a purpose and you don't love it, remove it! I do this all the time in my home, and I've coached several moms to do the same. You'll feel less stressed and spend far less time cleaning. I've noticed a lot of moms who claim to be overwhelmed have too much physical clutter around.

One time, I decluttered a friend's house to help her out, and she told me she felt like I'd given her a fresh start. She hadn't realized just how much the mess had impacted her life. Having too much stuff makes a home feel chaotic, and this in turn clutters your mind. Try reducing your material possessions by selling them, gifting them to family and friends, or giving them away to charity.

Tip #10 Buy Less Stuff

My rule of thumb when buying anything new is, *"Do I need this? Do I love this? Where will I put this?"* If I don't have the answers, I'll hold off buying it as it's best to live with less. The root of all clutter comes from over-spending and materialism. This is a disease of Western countries, where consumerism is heavily promoted as bringing joy and showing off one's affluence.

The vast selection of items out there makes us spend mindlessly on stuff we don't need. It's challenging to change a spending habit, but you won't go back once you do. When you live a clutter-free and minimalist lifestyle, your stress levels go waaaaay down, you clean less and have more time, and you have enough money to spend on things that matter.

Tip #11 Cut Down on Kitchen Prepping

Find easier ways to prepare meals. For example, when I buy certain vegetables for cooking (onions, carrots, spinach, kale, green peppers, celery, etc.), I buy them chopped up and frozen. This saves me so much time, money, and guilt. I discovered that the nutritional value of frozen fruit and vegetables is practically the same as fresh, plus they last longer, and it prevents those last-minute runs to the store.

I save time by not having to wash, drain, and chop vegetables before cooking a meal and it's frugal too. I find it cost effective because my vegetables don't end up rotten in the fridge because I forgot about them or didn't use them quickly enough.

When I cook certain meals, I don't always peel the skins off some vegetables (like potatoes and carrots). This is also a time saver and healthier, and my family hardly notices the difference. I try different hacks like boiling potatoes before adding them to the food, and using ready-mix spice packets to save on cooking time. So as you can see, you don't need be a slave to your kitchen, there are smarter, less time consuming ways to feed your family.

Tip #12 Cut Down Fussy Eating & Grazing

I don't allow my kids to be fussy eaters and it makes me cringe seeing children making demands on their poor mother. I hear kids saying, *"I don't eat this!"* and *"I don't eat that!"* or *"Take that off my plate!"* and it breaks my heart that they're being so ungrateful.

Don't allow your children to make such demands on you as they have no right to complain if you're feeding them tasty nutritional meals. The rule in my home is *"Eat it or leave it"* and *"There's no substitutions"* because I want my kids to appreciate our barakah and not feel entitled.

Also, don't allow your children to be grazers who eat all day long whenever they want. This is not only exhausting for a mother because of the never-ending clean-up, it's not a good way for anyone to eat. Assign specific mealtimes and ensure that your kids adhere to eating during those times which reduces eating out of boredom, overeating, and having a constant dirty kitchen.

Tip #13 Cook Easy Meals

Find recipes to make meals that don't have too many sides or preparation steps. Instead, cook meals that can be placed in one pot on the stove, as a dish in the oven, or in a fast or slow cooker. Some one-pot foods to make are; soups, goulashes, chili, stews, casseroles, pilafs, and curries.

I also use convenient appliances to save time on cooking like having an Instant Pot, pressure cooker, Crockpot and rice maker which saves hours of cooking time. Using helpful gadgets like an electric mixer and food chopper saves heaps of time on kitchen prepping.

I also keep a batch of pitas, tortillas, naan, rotis, and bread in the freezer, so I always have them on hand to warm-up when needed. You can always go back to making time-consuming meals if your family wants this, when you have less on your plate. Adopt the mindset, *"I'll do what I can when I can."*

Tip #14 Make Less Homemade Stuff

I know making homemade anything is a much better option and preferred by most families. I love homemade items best, whether it's food, beauty, or even cleaning products. However, it's not always possible for me to make them, and no one should feel guilty for not DIY-ing everything.

You don't *need* to bring a homemade dish to your friend's potluck if you can't manage it. It's perfectly okay to buy something instead, and if anyone takes issue with this, they've got the problem not you. No one has the right to judge another woman for such a minor issue as whether her food is homemade or bought from some place.

As long as it's halal, tastes decent, and moderately healthy, you do what you can without the embarrass-ment. I've taken items like fruit and salad trays, cakes and cookies, crackers and cheese trays with vegetables and dip, chocolate baskets, fruit punch, etc. to potlucks without feeling an ounce of guilt.

Sometimes when my family needs to invite a lot of people, we order food platters from a nice local restaurant to be less burdensome on us. There are times when we get unexpected guests and my husband and I will take the couple out for dinner instead of preparing a last minute meal. If they have kids, we order pizza for the little ones which makes the guests feel special and I don't dread having people over.

Tip #15 Give Your Kids Chores

I always urge parents to assign their kids chores, so if you haven't, try to remedy this as soon as possible. From a young age, my kids had to do both *basic* household chores and *personal* chores. Basic are things like setting the table, rinsing their plate, tidying the living room, etc. and personal are things like cleaning their bedroom, packing their laundry away, picking up their toys etc.

As kids get older, you can add on more challenging tasks that are appropriate for their age range. My teens now do things like clean and pack dishes, wash their dirty laundry, and clean their bathroom. I've noticed that many moms don't give their kids chores because they like things done a certain way or don't want to deal with the hassle.

For the former reason, you'll have to let go of your ideals and remind yourself that your home and belongings are just stuff. We won't take any of our material possessions to the grave, so why let it be such a big deal? For the latter reason, you'll need to take time to teach your children how to perform chores which takes heaps of patience, but the result will be rewarding in the long-run.

Tip #16 Reduce Cleaning Time

I take many shortcuts in my household chores when I don't have any cleaning help. I only clean areas of my home thoroughly only once a week, then do quick clean-ups throughout the week to maintain them. I also assign each of my kids a space to keep clean consistently to reduce the burden off me.

It helps to remove clean-up situations that never end such as, the constant wiping of tables and chairs, and sweeping after every mealtime. When my kids were all over five and under twelve years of age, we solved this problem by removing our dining furniture. We placed a rug on the floor with a tablecloth over so we could eat on the ground the Sunnah way.

During challenging times, I became ultra flexible and over the years I've tried different methods to avoid huge cleanups with my big family. I also highly recommend using easy cleaning supplies like a hand vacuum, spray mop, and having many spill clothes, wipes, and towels within easy reach.

Tip #17 Keep Things Simple

When times are tough, don't sweat the small stuff and keep things basic and uncomplicated. Don't burden yourself by maintaining unnecessary rules and rigor concerning your kids and home, and stop living for the unexpected guest. Choose a balanced approach like Islam promotes and take the route of simplicity and avoid materialism.

You'll see how much time you save when you focus more on what's important versus what's unnecessary for yourself and your family. I see mothers who fuss about what their children wear and how decorative their bedrooms are, having a guest-ready house with delicate ornaments, making elaborate meals that look exotic and cost a lot, etc.

Lose the high expectations and expensive lifestyle in place of focusing on life's simple pleasures like having a thriving family life and excellent health. Before we know it, precious time has passed, our children have grown-up and left, old age is diminishing our strength, and all the effort and money we put into our material possessions seem less appealing.

Tip #18 Have a Sense of Humor

Laugh when life is messy, chaotic, or just not going your way, and be okay laughing at yourself too. Humor has helped me put things into perspective even during the most challenging moments. Don't take everything so seriously with your husband and kids and be a tolerant and joyous woman – your family will love this about you!

If you need to loosen up a bit because over time, your responsibilities overtook your humor, start by watching a few comedies. As I mentioned before, some ways I keep my humor up is to watch funny YouTube videos, read humor quotes on Pinterest, message jokes and memes to my girlfriends, and share cute riddles with my kids. Life's short, so avoid being a "grumpy ol' mom" who's all about getting things done and not much fun to be around.

Tip #19 Limit Web & Social Media

Facebook, Twitter, Youtube, Instagram, Tik Tok, etc., whatever social media you're on, can be a time drain. In my humble opinion, it's something we can live without, especially if our days are crazy busy or it makes us feel worse.

There are benefits to using specific social platforms because you can learn a lot, get great recipes and craft ideas, and meet like-minded sisters. But sometimes, you can end up browsing too long and lose motivation because you become overwhelmed by so much content and choice.

If your social account is mainly filled with drama and adverts, it can make you feel sluggish and less productive. Even if there are a few informative posts here and there, the amount of time you spend and the mental toll it has on you ask yourself, "Is it worth it?"

At the very least, put a time limit on your social apps and lose the FMO (fear of missing out), which is a fallacy aimed at keeping you stuck. I speak from experience when I say that my life is much more wholesome since holding social media at arm's length and limiting the time spent on it.

As for turning to the web, it can be a great resource but also a huge distraction. I'll only touch my laptop when I have to do work or look up something important. Usually, we go online with a purpose, but along the way, we get distracted by reading something new or clicking a link, which leads to another link, and then another, until hours have passed.

Here's a tip that helped me when I struggled to balance my time online; commit to only browsing when you have something important to check. Stay disciplined, stick to that one search, and return only when you have another crucial goal to accomplish.

Tip #20 Remove Certain People From Your Life

Who needs fake friends and false relationships? I'm so grateful for real friends who are there to listen when I need to vent, or receive good advice when I have a problem. However, there were times I didn't have sincere friends and should've instead been alone than hung with sisters who were toxic to my life. Unfortunately, I trusted sisters sorely on whether they were practicing Muslimas.

I naively assumed that a sister in Islam could never want bad for another sister, but nowadays, you can't judge people on their faith alone. I had girlfriends, now ex-friends, who used me because they made me feel guilty if I didn't help them. I was naive about manipulative people and didn't realize how they try sneaky tactics to take advantage of you and care little about the time they're taking away from your family.

These types of "friends" can drain your energy and resources and are usually not there for you when you need them. Alhumdulillah, when I got older and wiser, I released myself from these friendships and noticed how my life got less stressful, I got closer to Allah SWT, and I also argued less with my husband and kids alhumdulillah.

Tip #21 Take Daily Time-Outs

The best way to declutter one's mind and get back on task is to find some peace and quiet to think. I started taking a time-out for ten to fifteen minutes as needed. I wasn't punishing myself like a kid; in reality, I was rewarding myself like an adult. We can become overwhelmed, forgetful, and far less productive when under pressure.

I know this isn't always possible with kids, but you'll need to explain to your children that mommy is feeling exhausted and needs to think for a few minutes (kids understand, and honesty works best).

I also ask my older kids to keep my younger kids busy by playing with them or reading them a story. I usually go to my bedroom, sit on my special musallah (prayer mat) with my back against the wall, close my eyes, and take deep breaths. As I calm my senses, I'll make some dhikr and let my tension and worries release. I don't take my laptop or phone with me because I want to focus and not feel distracted.

After about fifteen minutes, my head clears and my positive thoughts reappear. With this clarity, I know what needs to be accomplished and I start to make a mental plan with specific steps to get things done. This is also a good option when you feel angry or irritated with your children and want to avoid yelling and insulting them out of frustration.

Tip #22 Assign Yourself Some Personal Space

With young kids at home, everything you have is touched by little fingers. But let me warn you, older kids are just as bad! Not only do they start wearing your stuff, but they're into everything since gaining independence and doing most things on their own. I found this quite challenging as a mother who needed her private space where no child went.

At one time, when we had a bigger house and my kids were young, I converted a spare bedroom into "my office" and made it my personal area. No child was allowed to enter without permission, and I knew nothing would be touched when I put things in that room. Of course, I also had the option to lock the room when I wasn't using it which was an added bonus.

Now that we've moved to a smaller place and my kids are older, I can't have a private room to myself, so I've cornered-off a section of my bedroom, which is my "new office space." I have drawers and shelves that are "no-touch zones," and alhumdulillah, my children know and respect my boundaries. There'll be moments when one of my kids "borrows" something without asking, but it's pretty rare, and I don't make it a big deal because I accept it as part of mom life!

Tip #23 Make Yourself a Calm Spot

As I mentioned in my previous tip, if you don't have the space to create an "office" for yourself, find a small area of your home and claim it! This doesn't need to be an area where you work; it can simply be a "calm spot" where you don't allow your kids to play or put their stuff.

At my calm spot, the wall is lined with inspiring quotes and pretty art prints. I have my water bottle, some candles, and my favorite stationary supplies on my table. I place my journals and any books I like to read on a top shelf (which can be any single wall shelf). I make my spot feminine with a peaceful vibe. My kids even call it "mommy's tranquil space" and sometimes laugh at my quirky quotes, but they see how it brings me joy.

Tip # 24: Make Your Home Cozy

Not every house feels like a home, so making your home cozy is crucial. Fill your living spaces with warm, comfortable amenities and decor. You don't need to spend an arm and a leg to get a few items that bring warmth and comfort. I go to thrift stores and garage sales to shop for some housewares, and I often find lovely stuff which gives you the added delight of repurposing something used.

Mothers should make their homes a place where good memories are made and where it encourages love, positivity, and relaxation for their husbands and kids. We are the gatekeepers of our abode and when our home is thriving, it not only boosts your mood, but your family's mood as well. The saying "a woman's touch" is famous for a reason!

Tip #25 Journal For Comfort & Reflection

I'm a big proponent of journaling, and I've gone so far as to design journals for myself and offer them for sale. As a busy mother with a hectic life, I found that journaling my thoughts, goals, and dreams is hugely therapeutic. I recommend that moms do this as a regular habit and a way to brain dump their thoughts.

There's nothing like writing down your ideas on paper as a form of release, then turning your thoughts into actionable steps. Reflecting on your writing is also a great way to resolve a complex problem. Most importantly, I love to use journaling as a way to study Islam, keep up with my Quran and Hadith verses with the tafsir, and contemplate on Allah's SWT creation and names. It's one of my favorite de-stressors!

Tip #26 Do What You Love To Do

It may feel over said, but life's too short to spend it doing things you dislike. If it's in your means, pursue what you love doing as much as possible, and as wives, we have this luxury since we're not burdened with being the breadwinner alhumdullilah. This isn't to say you should overindulge in your dreams, but that you deserve to be rewarded for your hard work as a wife and mother. This makes you less resentful in the long-term. No matter what your individual tastes are, don't be afraid to give in once in a while and do things the more fun way.

For me, it's imperative that I do work I enjoy but also helps the ummah (Muslim community). I also eat foods I like in moderation instead of eating ample amounts of foods I don't love. Simply put, it's being gracious with yourself and knowing your likes and dislikes, so you become a woman who knows how to find and give joy.

Tip #27 Use a Meal Plan For Ease

You never want to get caught in a position where you haven't planned what to cook, you're bone-tired, and you lack the ingredients to make the family meal. Not only does the absence of good food make you more likely to give in to food cravings, but you could end up wasting money ordering junk food.

Now and then, it's fine to go that route, but when it becomes a habit, it's passed the point of moderation. To combat this problem, it's crucial to plan and prepare meals the day before at a minimum, but preferably a week in advance. If you can plan out a month's worth of meal plans, you should be officially crowned queen homemaker!

Meal plans are so highly beneficial and hugely reduce a mom's stress because it is one of the most dominant needs of the family, plus it helps them thrive and feel well looked after. I've designed a bunch of meal planning templates on my website at *zakeeyaali.com* if you don't want to create your own.

Tip #28 Use Scents For Pleasure

Your sense of smell has a tremendous effect on how you feel. Make it a point to accentuate your home with lovely fresh scents that are not complex or overwhelming. You can burn o'od or incense in your home or have a fragrant humidifier for essential oils. I boil orange peels with cinnamon sticks and cloves when I want to overcome a musty-smelling house or make it smell cozy in the autumn and winter seasons.

I also suggest you invest in a perfume you and your husband love. Spray on your favorite scent or women's atar every day when at home to feel luxurious and glamorous as a woman. I've been doing this for the longest time, and my husband and kids tell me that they love this about me and have fond memories of my constant sweet smell. It's such a confidence boost for a woman and even my girlfriends notice and compliment me about it.

Tip #29 Treat Yourself Like a Best Friend

Treating yourself as a best friend is a good way to get to know yourself without feeling conceited and arrogant. To do this, consider how you treat your best friend (I'm talking about your real friends, not your fake ones). When your girlfriend does something wrong, you're supportive and honest with her but in a kindly manner. When she does something right, you give her the kudos she deserves and become her biggest cheerleader.

You never insult or say hurtful things because it will break her down and make her sad. This is how you should treat yourself to prevent feeling resentful of others and to graciously forgive yourself for not being perfect. When you change your perspective to think of yourself as worthy, it will be harder to fall into self-loathing thought patterns, and you won't be your own worst enemy.

Tip #30 Spoil Yourself As You Deserve

Sometimes, indulge in something decadent, like a piece of chocolate or a small cup of coffee. Buy yourself something pretty to inspire you (like a journal). Once, I bought myself a pure leather wallet because it was something I had wanted for a long time but held off. After giving a lot to my family and home during a strenuous time, I felt that I deserved to gift myself a nice purse that I would use every day.

I didn't wait for anyone to guess my needs and gift something to me. Instead, I spoilt myself and felt oddly happy and giddy for a while. I know it may seem weird to gift yourself something if you've never done it before, but honestly, self-appreciation makes you confident and feel stronger to handle a busy life.

Tip #31 Beautify & Groom Yourself

You deserve to look and feel good, dear mom. Wear a pretty camisole underneath your blouse, put makeup on your face at home, moisturize your body, paint your finger and toe nails, design your hands and feet with henna, try a fresh haircut, dye your gray strands naturally, or all of the above!

If money is a concern, you can trim some hair bangs, wear a DIY face mask, exfoliate your body with a homemade sugar scrub, wax or shave your legs, or take a hot bath with bubbles or Epsom salts.

If you can afford it, I suggest occasionally getting a hairstyle at the hairdresser, going for a facial, pedicure, or a tension-releasing massage (my favorite). You can also buy some new face products or hijabs to raise your excitement and get out of your sweatpants rut.

I know it can be tough to feel motivated to groom when you have young kids and a chaotic household, but a little effort goes a long way. Besides looking delightful for your husband's pleasure (which is recommended in Islam), you should also do it for yourself. As a woman, you feel confident when you look and feel good, which in turn makes you more competent at your tasks.

I recommend watching Youtube videos to find hair, makeup, and clothing tutorials that suit you. Once you get your oomph back with some glamor grooming, your relationship with your husband may also get so much spicier!

Tip #32 Ask or Pay For Assistance

Don't be afraid to say, *"I need help."* I know I can do most things myself, but I would become exhausted and resentful by doing it all; plus, it isn't worth my well-being. I can say without guilt that when my six kids were young, I got weekly cleaning help for our home.

Many women feel guilty about hiring help for cleaning and cooking but are perfectly okay with getting a babysitter for their kids. You shouldn't feel guilty for wanting to spend time with your kids while someone else cleans and cooks for you. Learn to say, *"I need a hand because I'm not superwoman."*

If money is a concern, cut something else out of your budget. Most of the time, we can allocate a portion of our money when we regard a need as crucial. If you have tried to do things to de-stress but still feel under pressure, it may mean that your load is too much, and you can't proceed without getting some assistance.

In these cases, I always suggest hiring a mother's helper which is cheaper than a cleaner in the West, or ask your friend's teen daughter if she wants make some pocket money. A helper can assist you with some tasks once, twice, or thrice a week, depending on your budget and needs.

There is no shame in admitting you need help, and I speak from experience that getting a helper has really, really benefitted my health and family. I usually get someone to help with the housework instead of watch my children because I'd rather spend more time with my family than clean my house.

Tip #33 Use Technology At Your Convenience

Taking care of kids in today's world without devices is unrealistic. It's not impossible, but it's entirely dependent on your situation and the support you have around. As a mom of six living in the West with no extended family assistance and a husband who works a lot, I use technology at opportune times to get stuff done. If your situation is somewhat similar, I suggest using devices to work in your favor and with a balanced approach.

When I feel pressured by my children, I put on an appropriate show for them to watch so I can make calls, write emails, pay bills, or do some personal grooming. I'm not particularly eager to punish my kids from devices as a rule because I'm the one to suffer the most. Even if your child is a reader and has hobbies, these days, it's tough to keep children completely offline because most schools require the web unless you live an alternative lifestyle.

I remember using encyclopedias to research when I was a kid, but nowadays, teachers want students to do their assignments on a computer. Thus my husband and I are more focused on *what* our children watch and how much time they use, than avoiding technology altogether. Don't feel guilty for using it as an occasional sitter especially if you don't generally allow your kids use devices mindlessly; use the time they're on a device to your advantage. If your kids are older and it's a couple of hours of educational content, it isn't a big deal.

Of course, the younger your kids, the less you should let them be in front of a screen, and I don't recommend that infants and toddlers use devices because they're bad for their brain development. Also, your kids don't need to watch TV or play video games; there's also the option for them to listen to audiobooks and Islamic rhymes. In this way, you can add more time since it's not visual, so you can get your tasks done.

Tip #34 Pick Up Hobbies

Women who have hobbies are much happier because they spend their spare time creating and honing in on their skills. Pursuing hobbies can be a form of de-stressing for many people, and it doesn't have to be hectic or scheduled; it just has to bring you some joy.

For example, one of my friends loves to craft things from odds and ends and goes to dollar stores to buy her supplies. She'll make lovely gifts for friends and family, which gives her so much fulfillment. Another friend loves to garden and make her own edible and non-edible products. She gets satisfaction when she cooks from her garden's vegetables and feels joy from making her body potions.

Working on our passions as women, can bring us a lot of contentment, and making something with your hands can be highly comforting. Simply think of what you enjoy doing the most, collect your supplies, and start from there.

Tip #35 Get Adequate Sleep

Remember, you can't pour from an empty cup. If you're sleep-deprived, you won't be able to wake up each day to be the best version of yourself and see to your family with a smile. Many studies show how lack of sleep negatively affects your mind and body and makes one unable to concentrate and focus.

I always think of resting for my body's sake and sleeping for my mind's sake. When I don't prioritize sleep, I'm not the only one who feels the consequences because everyone around me also has to deal with my short patience. To ward off crankiness and burnout from lack of rest, I'll turn down social invitations, reschedule appointments, avoid the TV and PC, and put down my phone in favor of catching up on sleep.

For example, if your baby is teething and keeps you up at night, you'll need to make up for lost sleep. Your husband or helper can watch the kids for a few hours in the day while you catch-up on sleep. If you have older kids, you can rest when your kids nap or set up a quiet time for them to read or make floor puzzles in their bedroom.

If you cannot find the time due to your schedule being too full, you'll need to cut some things out that may be less important. When a woman feels tired all the time, the last thing she feels like doing is taking care of herself, which deepens her slump and becomes a vicious cycle of demotivation.

Tip #36 Go On Outings Alone

When my kids were young, I used to go out alone at least once a week to do errands. I did this usually on weekends when my husband was home, so he'd see to our kids. When I didn't do this consistently, I stopped getting "alone time," and my mood became less chipper. Even now, with my kids being older and their demands greater, I still get overwhelmed when I don't get time away for myself

If your situation doesn't allow you to go out and take a break, designate a time once a week at home to relax when your kids are at school. If you homeschool, your kids are always around, so getting some alone time is even more critical. You can enroll your kids in extra-curricular classes, exchange childcare with friends, or get your eldest child to babysit. Taking time off for yourself as a woman ensures you have balance because you'll feel you have a life by setting time aside for your needs.

Tip #37 Listen To Quran & Inspirational Tunes

The Quran is healing, and it will comfort you beyond imagination. Whenever my home is in turmoil, or I feel stressed out by my life, I'll play my favorite qari (reciter) on the TV. I usually do this via Youtube in the mornings, so my kids and I can read the translation over beautiful scenery as we complete our chores.

I especially love playing parts of sura Baqarah over a few days as this also removes the shayateen from one's home for days. After playing the recitation of the Quran, I immediately notice my patience returns, and tranquility fills our home. It's sakina in its truest form!

You can also play uplifting nasheeds for a happy vibe, and young kids love this. One of the quickest ways to get out of a bad mood or let go of sadness is to go for a drive and play some motivational Islamic songs in the car; this has made me feel better in no time.

Tip #38 Get a Cat For Comfort If You Like Pets

As a busy mom, the last thing you want is to have something else to take care of. This is a fair sentiment, and initially, I didn't want my kids to have any pet other than fish when they desperately wanted a cat. I love cats but wasn't a fan of getting one due to my responsibilities. But my kids kept begging their dad, until he came home with three kittens one day.

I remember thinking, *"OMG, how am I going to cope?!"* But Allah SWT is great, and when your intentions are good, he brings barakah to your life. My husband had saved the kittens from a shelter, and alhumdulillah, our cats are well-mannered, have become an essential part of our family, and bring my children a lot of joy.

I didn't expect our cats to bring me such comfort and calm too. They'll console me when I feel sad, and stroking them is truly relaxing. I've discovered that cats can pick up on human emotions, and even serve as therapy pets for patients in hospital.

If you can get a cat for your home, I recommend it, because cats can be an incredible source of solace for mothers and make great companions for you children. The added benefits are that cats are quiet and clean, so they're super easy to maintain!

Tip #39 Play Soothing Frequencies or Calming Sounds

External sounds have a remarkable impact on the human brain. I'm no expert on the subject, but if you look up the benefits of specific frequencies, you'll learn how they can vastly affect your mood. Personally, I prefer to occasionally play in the background sounds with ocean waves, a waterfall, or rainfall from a Youtube video for a relaxing vibe.

When I'm stressed out and my home is noisy, I'll also put on headphones and play calm sounds from my PC instead of yelling at my kids to be quiet. This instantly drowns out the chaos and helps me to unwind from the turmoil. There are hundreds of compilations on YouTube to peruse, but I recommend searching for peaceful music or nature sounds, two of my favorites, to refocus and feel serene amidst the storm of a rambunctious family life.

Tip #40 Set Aside Relaxation Time

My mentor made me realize that my definition of relaxation was utterly wrong. Despite taking time for myself, I would still feel excessively drained. I was shown that absolute relaxation is doing something I liked but didn't necessarily mean something I derived benefit from. For example, in my spare time, I would write articles for my website, fix technical issues, post on social media, and answer messages.

I thought my hobby was having "me-time" because I wasn't doing anything for my kids or home. But in reality, I was still seeing the needs of others, so I didn't feel rested because I wasn't taking time for *my* needs. Even though I was passionate about my work, it still took a toll on me.

I had to learn that in order to feel relaxed, you are supposed to do something that refreshes and reboots you so you're energized to tackle your tasks again. This would be something that's not hectic, has no deadline, and is purely done to unwind.

Tip #41 Reconnect With Your Husband

You don't need to do anything hectic to connect with dear hubby. Trying to get him to go on date nights or urging him to buy you gifts won't rekindle your love for one another.

Instead, tell your husband what you would love to do with him or do something you both enjoy for the simple reason of spending time together. It's more essential to have a strong marriage when you have kids because if your relationship is thriving, you can handle parenting a lot better.

Many women neglect their husbands when they become mothers, thinking they're just too busy to be supportive wives. What ends up happening is your husband pulls away due to this neglect, and your parenting journey becomes much more challenging without his support. When you give time to your spouse, and you're respectful and trusting of his abilities as a father, he'll feel needed and do so much more to help the family succeed.

Tip #42 Reconnect With Your Kids

If you're with your kids a lot, you may think it's adequate, but it's about choosing quality over quantity time. Being with your children the entire day is not the same as doing something with them during the day. Instead, give each of your kids a good fifteen minutes of one-on-one time a few times a week, or even an hour once a week.

Children often don't know how to handle their emotions, so they act out without realizing why. When I notice my young child whining or throwing a tantrum, or see my teen acting moody and irritable, I know I need to give them one-on-one time. I then close what I'm doing to have a chat, give a hug, or look into their eyes to ask if everything's okay. I try to also crack jokes or share some humor to make them laugh as a fast fix.

I assure you that you'll see a difference in your child's attitude after ten minutes. You have fewer problems when you spend quality time with your children, because kids act out when they seek attention and validation. Also as a mother, you'll feel connected to your child and won't get mom guilt for not knowing what they're up to or wondering if you're spent enough time with them.

Tip #43 Socialize With Good Girlfriends

Having girlfriends to talk to is essential, and regular chats with your sister or a good friend can be very therapeutic. Face-to-face interaction is still best, but nowadays unfortunately, it's not always possible.

As a busy parent, you handle problems all day long, and the never-ending loop can make you feel like a hamster on a wheel. Being in the company of uplifting women significantly boosts your well-being, but you must be wary of unhealthy friendships as they can be worse than being alone.

When I moved to a new city some time ago, I didn't know anyone, which made me feel down. As soon as I committed to attending some social functions and saw new faces, I was on my way to feeling much better. Sometimes, even getting the kids ready for a playdate with other moms seems daunting but it's worth it when you make the effort.

For this reason, whenever I feel doubt creep up about going for a meetup, I think how much better I always feel, that I tend to learn something new, and sometimes meet a friend along the way. I know that the trip will be beneficial more often than not, so I need to stop overthinking it.

You can always learn from others; no matter who they are or where they're from, there will always be something you didn't know. Socializing is an innate part of being human, and we go against our very nature if we become a recluse who's wrapped up in oneself, hiding from the rest of society.

Tip #44 Be Charitable & Give Gifts

When you give to others, you feel good inside, and the reason is that giving gifts and offering sadaqa is a Sunnah! Acts of charity bring barakah to your life and help take the focus off your worries to think of the plight of others.

From my experience, the women I know who are happy and grateful are very generous. The ones who constantly complain and feel depressed seem always to be looking for handouts. A clear difference between those that give and those that take.

I will often try to give some charity here and there to those in need or an organization I trust. I don't worry if it's a small amount as I do what I can afford and the intention is to help from whatever means you have. I also gift my girlfriends with small crafts I make, add some chocolates to a pretty gift bag with ribbon, or write a sweet note. I love it when my friends do the same for me as it strengthens our bonds of love and care of one another.

I do the same for my husband and kids and I don't focus on giving expensive gifts, but to gift them things they would use often. I aim to only give to others with the intention of fisabilillah (for Allah's sake) and without expecting anything in return so I can gain the maximum reward and keep my intentions pure.

Tip #45 Take Naps When You Need Rest

Islam propagates the importance of qailulah (midday rest), which is part of the Sunnah. Scientific evidence supports it, claiming daily napping is conducive to total relaxation and sleep. Many moms I know don't take advantage of this and can't fathom sleeping in the daytime. Despite this, I recommend you try it at least once to see the benefits.

You don't need to nap where you fall asleep, you can also lie down on the bed and relax for 15–30 minutes. Taking a brief sleep is called a "power nap" because it helps you feel more productive, not groggy, and doesn't disrupt your bedtime. You can take naps with your younger kids or when your older kids are at school. If you homeschool as I do, set up a specific time for everyone to be quiet and insist that this is "chill time" where mommy needs time to relax.

Tip #46 Pray Tahajjud For Relief

In my times of distress, I've found tahajjud salah to be my salvation. Imam Ash Shafi R.A said;

> **"The dua made at tahajjud is like an arrow that does not miss its target."**

The Prophet SAW said;

> **"The best prayer after the obligatory prayers is the night prayer." (Muslim)**

Tahajjud has increased my stamina, strengthened my heart, and left me feeling tranquil. When you begin implementing tahajjud in your life, you'll feel like you have an extra coat of armor against the world as a wife and mother. People and situations will not trigger you like they usually would, and sabr will come naturally. I've done research on tahajjud and wrote an extensive article which you can read on my website at *zakeeyaali.com.*

Tip #47 Turn To Daily Dua For Allah's SWT Help

When I say my morning adkhar, my day runs as smooth as butter, my problems seem lighter, and my resilience is higher when dealing with challenges. Dua is that extra safety measure of seeking Allah's SWT assistance for yourself and all you have going on in your life. So why not take advantage of this shield that our Lord sent us to deal with the dhuniya's trials?

I make dua for many things I can't control as a woman. When I'm worried about my child going somewhere or pursuing an adventurous goal, I have learned to turn to Allah SWT instead of worrying until my head hurts. Dua helps you let go of thinking you have control over the safety of your life and your family and instead put all your trust and belief that only our Creator keeps us safe.

It really lessens your daily worry about the things out of your hands and keeps you sane on the days you feel like breaking down in distress. I urge every Muslim to learn the morning and evening adkhar in their language, so it's understandable and not hectic. I have an app on my phone called the *Dhikr & Dua* app, which is free, devoid of adverts, grants easy access to many supplications for every facet of life, and includes Hadith references.

Tip #48 Don't Be Everyone's Shoulder To Cry On

You can't be present for everyone in your life, and you definitely cannot correspond with everyone you've ever met. Smartphones and social media have made the world seem smaller, and we have access to people we would've never kept in contact with. It's impossible to be on every online platform and constantly calling and texting with so many people.

At one time, I was burning out from having so many friends that I had to let go of communicating with some of them after realizing how many hours I spent responding to messages. One day I finally I said, *"Enough!"* and decided to do what I could when I could and to stop worrying about what people thought of me. If those friends didn't understand that I had a lot on my plate, like seeing to my husband and six kids, homeschooling, plus working part-time, they were not the friends I needed in my life.

The other thing I realized was the more friends I made, the more emotional baggage I took on. I had to offer each one of them my support and sometimes I couldn't keep up with the different problems they faced and remembering to check-in often. I felt the burden of proving I cared and was making dua for them when I had so much on my plate.

I know it sounds crass to say this, but the reality is that it's impossible to be present to so many people and we were never meant to. Making dua for your extended family and friends has more clout anyway, but many people don't appreciate this and want to hear your niceties so it can become draining.

Tip #49 Only Put Your Heart & Hopes On Allah SWT

I learned many years ago not to put my heart on anyone but Allah SWT. This isn't to say that I don't *need* anyone or don't *care* about my loved ones; it simply means I don't *love* anyone more than Him. It sounds simple, but it's not an easy state of mind to adopt as we want instant gratification and affirmation from our loved ones.

To achieve this, you must let go of those you love to a certain extent in your heart. The reason it's essential is that every single person will disappoint you, except Allah SWT. Our Lord wants us to depend on Him entirely and not on anyone or anything more. However, sometimes we do the opposite and place our trust, for example, in a doctor or medication to give our child relief for their ailment. Instead, we should be first turning to the healing verses of the Quran and our sincere words of dua asking our Lord, Ash-Shifa to heal us.

Sometimes we wonder how people can be so hurtful and cruel, but maybe that's Allah SWT showing us how flawed people are and that only He is perfect and our only savior. When you stop putting your heart in the wrong place, like on your spouse, kids, parents, friends etc., you'll also feel more empowered! You'll be protected from disappointment and betrayal, which means you may still get hurt but you won't break apart, and that's a healthy state of mind to have.

Tip #50 Strengthen Your Faith & Be Patient

Last but not least, have faith in the Qadr of Allah SWT. Know that He doesn't give a soul more than they can bear.

> **"Allah does not charge a soul except (with that within) its capacity. It will have (the consequence of) what (good) it has gained, and it will bear [the consequence of] what (evil) it has earned." (Quran 2:286)**

That's why we say the dua:

"Our Lord, do not impose blame upon us if we have forgotten or erred. Our Lord, and lay not upon us a burden like that which You laid upon those before us. Our Lord, and burden us not with that which we have no ability to bear. And pardon us; and forgive us; and have mercy upon us. You are our protector, so give us victory over the disbelieving people." (Quran 2:286)

Alongside your faith, have patience about the difficulties you can't control. Allah SWT says:

"O you who have believed, seek help through patience and prayer. Indeed, Allah is with the patient." (Quran 2:153)

Remind yourself that every single sacrifice you make, especially as a mother, is immensely rewarded. We must understand the need to strive for our goals and that *nothing great is easy to achieve*. We should apply this mindset towards our wifehood and motherhood and regard it as our ticket to Jannah inshallah. Imagine our

endurance when we're able to set our focus straight towards the akhira instead of the dhuniya!

Recap of 50 Tips To Survive Motherhood

1. Wake up earlier than everyone else.

2. Write down everything and categorize it.

3. Prioritize your duties to avoid overwhelm.

4. Become organized even if you don't enjoy it.

5. Implement routines and structure.

6. Time your tasks.

7. Bookmark and use sticky notes.

8. Remain consistent in what you do.

9. Declutter your stuff.

10. Buy less stuff.

11. Cut down on kitchen prepping.

12. Cut down fussy eating and grazing.

13. Cook easier meals.

14. Make less homemade stuff.

15. Give your kids chores.

16. Reduce cleaning time.

17. Keep things simple.

18. Have a sense of humor.

19. Limit web and social media.

20. Remove certain people from your life.

21. Take daily time-outs.

22. Assign yourself some personal space.

23. Make yourself a calm spot.

24. Make your home cosy.

25. Journal for comfort and reflection.

26. Do what you love to do.

27. Use a meal plan for ease.

28. Use scents for pleasure.

29. Treat yourself like a best friend.

30. Spoil yourself as you deserve.

31. Beautify and groom yourself.

32. Ask or pay for assistance.

33. Use technology at your convenience.

34. Pick up hobbies.

35. Get adequate sleep.

36. Go on outings alone.

37. Listen to Quran and inspirational tunes.

38. Get a cat for comfort if you like pets.

39. Play soothing frequencies or calming sounds.

40. Set aside relaxation time.

41. Reconnect with your husband.

42. Reconnect with your kids.

43. Socialize with good girlfriends.

44. Be charitable and give gifts.

45. Take naps when you need rest.

46. Pray tahajjud for guaranteed relief.

47. Turn to daily dua for Allah's SWT help.

48. Don't be everyone's shoulder to cry on.

49. Only put your heart and hopes on Allah SWT.

50. Strengthen your faith and be patient.

Conclusion

Alhumdulillah, you've made it to the end of this book. I pray you'll look at mom life more positively since discovering how to manage your responsibilities and feel more joyful doing it. It may take some time for you to reach this point, so please don't lose hope, as it's a continuous journey of improvement.

I feel blessed to have completed this book for mothers with the tips that helped me during my years of overwhelm and reaching a state of tranquility. It pains me to see so many moms suffering in their roles since I know it's not how motherhood should be, as there are things we can do to solve our troubles.

As mentioned in my chapters, by fully accepting your motherhood challenges, knowing your sacrifices are immensely rewarded, and realizing the value you bring, will help you endure many tough parenting days. And once you consciously change your mindset for the better, start losing the traits that keep you stuck in the grind, and set better standards for yourself, your overwhelm will significantly dissipate and maybe disappear!

Putting all of this into practice will be difficult at the beginning, but over time it will give you the strength to overcome resentment, impatience, frustration, and feeling discouraged. The Prophet PBUH SAW,

"Allah does not look at your figures, nor at your attire, but He looks at your hearts and accomplishments." (Muslim)

Journaling your progress, whether in a notebook or using the companion *Tranquil Muslim Wife Reflection Journal,* will help you derive the benefits of this book so you can effectively incorporate the principles in your life. However, if your responsibilities are still causing you anguish, don't ignore your feelings! It might mean that your responsibilities are more than your capabilities.

In this case, you'll need to make significant adjustments to your situation because no mother should live with high-stress levels and accept this as "a fact of life." Yes, now and again, challenging times are unavoidable, and we all deal with life's turmoil as this is the nature of the dhuniya. But when you mostly feel like you're losing it or at the end of your rope, that not a healthy state.

Remember, the definition of insanity is to do the same thing over and over, expecting different results.

No mother should suffer in silence, so if you can't change your circumstance alone, I advise you to get support from an expert. I offer mentoring for mothers who need tailored support at *zakeeyaali.com/coaching* if you'd like to work with me, but there are many coaches online who can help. I've used a mentor myself and therefore recommend finding a good one to solve your non-traumatic situation as they will advise you compared to therapists who diagnose and medicate.

Of course, there is no quick fix if you're in a challenging situation requiring drastic change, but the first important step is acknowledging you need help. Then, you'll need to set aside the time and commit to implementing what you've learned to see it through. I can promise you the results are well worth the effort!

If you know of a sister or friend going through a tough mom life, recommend this book and try doing the tips together as a team. I tried this one time with a good friend and a book I liked, and the collective brainstorming and accountability were very effective. You can also start a book club and have a sisters' discussion group, which I like because you can hear different perspectives.

Lastly, don't only read this book once and forget it on your bookshelf. I read certain books repeatedly because I forget the concepts and take them as a continual guide. I'll highlight important paragraphs and use sticky flag notes to bookmark relevant pages for later reference.

Keep up the faith, my dear fellow mom; I know you can do this! May Allah SWT grant you ease and success in your motherhood journey, ameen.

Inspiration

Peace. It does not mean to be in a place where there is no noise, trouble or hard work. It means to be in the midst of those things and still, be calm in your heart. - Anonymous

Being a mother is learning about strengths you didn't know you had, and dealing with fears you didn't know existed. – Linda Wooten

Special Duas For Moms

When times are tough, dua is our salvation. Many of us don't use it to our advantage or realize the gift we have at our disposal from our Most Merciful Lord. Ask Him for the comfort you need on your motherhood journey always. Allah SWT listens to our requests and promises to answer them, especially as parents.

Here are two examples of duas I say regularly that you may like to add to your daily supplications. One is where I'm asking for ease as a mother and for my children's future happiness, and the other is asking for help to cope and for my children to be easy to raise. May Allah SWT accept our duas, ameen.

A Dua For Motherhood Ease and Comfort For Children

"O Allah, grant me, righteous children who will find righteous spouses, and have righteous children of their own. And make my spouse and offspring the coolness of my eyes." Ameen

A Dua For Motherhood Ease From Exhaustion and Stress

"O Allah, grant me the ability to cope on my motherhood journey, relieve me of my struggles, and make my children righteous, compassionate, and successful in this life and the next." Ameen

From The Author's Desk

Thank you for purchasing *Tranquil Muslim Mom - How To Find Serenity as a Mother and Cope With Overwhelm*. You can also purchase the accompanying, *Tranquil Muslim Mom Personal Reflection Journal* to reflect on the tips discussed in the book.

I pray this read has benefitted you and granted you more insight into being a more peaceful and calmer mom. Look for the next book in my series, *Tranquil Muslim Wife*, to complete your journey of achieving serenity and to learn even more valuable tips towards becoming a contented wife and mother.

If you enjoyed this book and it helped you, I'd really appreciate your review on Amazon or drop me a comment at *hello@zakeeyaali.com* – I promise to respond. Your valuable feedback and suggestions help me know what wives and moms of today are thinking and what content they want more of.

I also appreciate your amanah (trust) by not sharing the digital version of this book with others, as much time and research went into writing and publishing it. Jazakallah khair for your support.

Peace Be Upon You, Zakeeya Ali

About The Author

Zakeeya Ali is a South African-born Muslima and the fourth child of five siblings. She has been a wife to her American husband and a mother to her children for over 20 years, alhumdulillah.

She majored in Psychology, Sociology, and Information Science and worked as an elementary teacher for a few years. The profound loss of her parents and youngest brother early in life, reminded her of the temporary nature of this world and inspired her to help others.

She founded her website, *zakeeyaali.com* (formerly Muslimommy), in 2011, when she discovered a niche for supporting Muslim spouses and parents living in challenging modern societies. She's passionate about spreading traditional Islamic values towards our roles as wives and mothers and reviving our fitra as Muslim women.

She currently resides in the USA with her husband, six children, and three cats and is proud to be a full-time stay-at-home mom who has been homeschooling her kids for over a decade. She works part-time as a mentor, author, and designer, and you'll find her publications of journals at *muslimjournals.com* and her books and services at *zakeeyaali.com*.

Also By The Author

If you would like to know more about the author, or where to follow her, and purchase her other products, find the links to all her work, socials, and books below.

Web Links

- **zakeeyaali.com** - The author's main website.

- **muslimjournals.com** - The author's website for Islamic journaling and reflection.

- **islamichomeeducation.com** - The author co-founded this website for parents to teach their kids beneficial knowledge.

Social Media

- **@zakeeyaali on Twitter** - Where the author frequently tweets.

- **@zakeeyaali on Pinterest** - Where the author hosts an array of helpful boards.

- **@zakeeyaali on Youtube** - Where the author posts informative videos and shorts.

Books and Journals For Adults

1. Tranquil Muslim Mom Reflection Journal

2. Tranquil Muslim Mom, Memories of My Children Journal

3. Tranquil Muslim Wife Book

4. Tranquil Muslim Wife Reflection Journal

5. Tranquil Muslim Wife, Memories of My Husband Journal

6. Teach Your Child Salah and Make It Stick!

7. When Your Child Lies, Ways To Help You Cope!

8. A Muslima's Personal Dua Book and Journal

9. Quran Journal

10. Hadith Journal

11. Dua Journal

12. Daily Dua Journal

13. Asma ul Husna Journal

14. Salah Journal

15. Sawm Journal

16. Ramadan Journal

17. Shukr Journal

18. Barakah Journal

19. Niyyah Journal

20. Halaqa Journal

Books, Ebooks and Journals For Kids

1. My Quran Journal

2. My Hadith Journal

3. My Dua Journal

4. My Asma ul Husna Journal

5. My Salah Journal

6. My Ramadan Journal

7. My Shukr Journal

8. My Niyyah Journal

9. Let's Learn About Muharram

10. Let's Learn About The Hijri Months

11. The Hijri Calendar

12. The Battle of Karbala

13. The Day of Ashura

14. Tremendous Character Like The Prophet SAW

15. The Prophet's SAW Mannerisms

IMPORTANT NOTES

IMPORTANT NOTES

IMPORTANT NOTES

IMPORTANT NOTES

IMPORTANT NOTES

IMPORTANT NOTES

Our Lord! Grant that our spouses and our offspring be a comfort to our eyes, and give us the grace to lead those who are conscious of You. (Quran 25:74)

Jazakallah khair for purchasing this book.

Made in United States
Troutdale, OR
02/22/2024

17872052R10159